KAREN BROWN'S

Italy

Charming Bed & Breakfasts

Karen Brown Titles

Austria: Charming Inns & Itineraries

California: Charming Inns & Itineraries

England: Charming Bed & Breakfasts

England, Wales & Scotland: Charming Hotels & Itineraries

French Country Bed & Breakfasts

France: Charming Inns & Itineraries

Germany: Charming Inns & Itineraries

Ireland: Charming Inns & Itineraries

Italy: Charming Bed & Breakfasts

Italy: Charming Inns & Itineraries

Spain: Charming Inns & Itineraries

Swiss Country Inns & Itineraries

KAREN BROWN'S
Italy
Charming Bed & Breakfasts

Written by

NICOLE FRANCHINI

Illustrations by Elisabetta Franchini

Cover Painting by Jann Pollard

Travel Press
Karen Brown's Country Inn Series

Editors: Nicole Franchini, Clare Brown, June Brown, Karen Brown, Iris Sandilands
Technical support: William H. Brown III; Aide-de-camp: William H. Brown

Illustrations: Elisabetta Franchini, Cover painting: Jann Pollard, Cover design: Tara Brassil
Maps: Susanne Lau Alloway—Greenleaf Design & Graphics

Written in cooperation with Carlson Wagonlit/Town & Country Hillsdale Travel, San Mateo, CA 94401

Distributed USA & Canada: The Globe Pequot Press; tel: (860) 395-0440, fax: (860) 395-0312
Box 833, Old Saybrook, CT 06475-0833, USA

Distributed Europe: Springfield Books Ltd.; tel: (01484) 864 955, fax: (01484) 865 443
Norman Road, Denby Dale, Huddersfield HD8 8TH, W. Yorkshire, England

Distributed Australia & New Zealand: Little Hills Press Pty. Ltd.
Tel: (02) 437-6995, fax: (02) 438-5762
1st Floor, Regent House, 37-43 Alexander St, Crows Nest NSW 2065, Australia

A catalog record for this book is available from the British Library

Library of Congress Cataloging-in-Publication Data

Franchini, Nicole, 1959-
    Karen Brown's Italy : charming bed & breakfasts / written by
Nicole Franchini ; illustrations by Elisabetta Franchini ; cover
painting by Jann Pollard. -- Totally rev 3rd ed.
        p. cm. -- (Karen Brown's country inn series)
    Includes index.
    ISBN 0-930328-35-3 (pb)
    1. Bed and breakfast accommodations--Italy--Guidebooks. 2. Italy-
-Guidebooks.   I. Title. II. Series.
TX907.5.I8F73 1996
647.9445'03--dc20   95-16413
                                                                        CIP

To
Carlo and Livia,
With all my Love

ITALIAN FARMER'S POEM

Our memories are crouched
in silence within the belly of the earth.
Yet it takes only a day of sunshine,
an impromptu storm in the sky,
the perfume of freshly cut hay,
and immense fields dotted with golden haystacks,
to ignite in us the memories
of certain evenings spent full of gaiety.

It was at sunset when we used to join together
in the barn filled with grain
to celebrate the end of the harvest.
The "gioanassa" musician friend,
pressing the keys of his worn-out accordion,
succeeding in emitting the notes
to a waltz or mazurka, leaving us
drunk with happiness.

One more glass of wine before the night
fades into day.
One more toast to bid farewell
to another summer
that crossed the path of our youth.

Anonymous

Contents

Introduction

BED AND BREAKFAST ITALIAN-STYLE—*agriturismo*, as the bed and breakfast activity is called in Italy, has made great strides over the past decade. The bed and breakfast concept is relatively new to Italy, which followed suit after France and England originated the trend. Accommodations vary from simple farmhouses to noble country villas, all promising unique and memorable stays. *"Agritourism"* travel offers visitors to Italy the unique opportunity to observe daily life "up close" as a guest in someone's home. It is a superb way to interact directly with Italians, experiencing their way of life as a participant rather than just an observer. It offers a more intimate contact with the country's traditional ways of life than can ever be experienced during hotel stays. It is the alternative vacation for curious visitors who wish to explore the back roads of this fascinating country and depart with a more in-depth understanding of Italians and their lifestyles than they could possibly get from city stays and sightseeing alone. The individual who will benefit most from agritourism will have an open, inquiring mind and a certain amount of flexibility. In return, agritourism rewards the traveler with a feeling of being "at home" while abroad. The warm welcome and the value you'll receive will tempt you back to the agritourism track year after year.

HISTORY: *Agriturismo*, defined as agricultural tourism, was launched in 1965 as part of the Italian government's national agricultural department's plan to make it possible for farmers to supplement their declining income in two ways: through offering accommodation to tourists and through direct sales of their produce.

After World War II, during reconstruction and the subsequent industrial boom, Italians abandoned the countryside in droves in search of employment in urban centers, reducing the rural population from eight to three million people. Consequently, farmhouses, villas, and castles all across the country were neglected and went to ruin. This phenomenon also disrupted the centuries-old tradition of passing customs and property from one generation to the next.

The agritourism concept, with its government funding, proclaimed tax breaks, and an increasing need to escape congested cities, has lured proprietors back to their land and ancestral homes, providing them with the incentive to restore and preserve these historical buildings (with many treasures among them), without spoiling the natural landscape. An additional consequence is an improved distribution of tourism between Italy's overcrowded cities and the countryside which serves to raise awareness of the many marvelous historical and cultural attractions, from art and architecture to scenery and cuisine, that await tourists off the beaten track.

Each of Italy's 20 regions participates in agritourism, with a full 60% of participants concentrated in Tuscany and Trentino-Alto Adige. This third edition of *Italy: Charming Bed & Breakfasts* includes selections from 14 of Italy's regions. Unfortunately, this type of accommodation is still very scarce in Italy's southernmost regions such as Calabria,

Basilicata, and Campania. A selection of nine bed and breakfasts in Sicily, where a new law permitting agritourism activity has just been passed, is featured in this edition.

In practical terms, agritourism was developed to stimulate the local economy in rural areas by encouraging the creation of accommodation (rooms, apartments, and campgrounds) in places where they had never before been available. In a more long-term and idealistic sense, it was hoped that the promotion and development of tourism in rural Italy would also bring about greater environmental awareness and rescue traditional folklore and customs, such as regional cuisine and handicrafts, from oblivion.

For Italians, agritourism facilitates an exchange of views between farmers and urbanites who come in search of a peaceful vacation surrounded by natural beauty. In fact, agritourism and the rich culture of the farmer represent for many an affirmation and validation of their heritage. Lamentably, some Italians still have a misconception of agritourism because it was originally organized as an exchange of very basic room and board for work in the fields. A wave of positive press in the past three years and higher quality standards have helped enormously to change this outdated image.

Controversy also surrounds the fact that there are few established regulations governing this type of activity, and they differ greatly from one region to another. Consequently, no clearly defined quality standards exist and those participants with limited economic resources resent wealthier proprietors, whom they accuse of running accommodations resembling hotels more than farm stays.

Moreover, it does not simplify matters that agritourism is organized in typical Italian fashion, with responsibility divided among three associations, each with its own regulations, politics, and guidelines. Each association produces a directory (in Italian) and may be contacted by writing to:

AGRITURIST, Corso Vittorio Emanuele 101, Rome 00168, Italy

TERRANOSTRA, Via 14 Maggio 43, Rome 00187, Italy

TURISMO VERDE, Via E. Franceschini 89, Rome 00155, Italy

About Bed & Breakfasts

Our goal in this guide is to recommend outstanding places to stay. All of the bed and breakfasts featured have been visited and selected solely on their merits. Our judgments are made on charm, setting, cleanliness, and, above all, warmth of welcome. No bed and breakfast ever pays to be included. However (no matter how careful we are), sometimes we misjudge an establishment's merits, or the ownership changes, or unfortunately sometimes standards are not maintained. If you find a recommended place is not as we have indicated, please let us know, and accept our sincere apologies. The rates given are those quoted to us by the bed and breakfast: please use these figures as a guideline and be certain to ask at the time of booking what the rates are and what they include.

ACCOMMODATION

The most important thing to remember as you consider an agritourism vacation is that you will be staying in the private homes of families that are obligated to run their bed and breakfasts without hiring additional personnel aside from family and farmhands. Do not forget that, in most cases, the primary responsibility of your hosts is the running of their farm, so, with a few exceptions, do not expect the service of a hotel. Rooms are not always cleaned daily (sometimes rooms are cleaned only every three days). Nevertheless, do anticipate a comfortable and enjoyable stay, because the proprietors will do everything possible to assure it. Cost will vary according to the level of service offered. (For the traveler's convenience, some city hotels have been included that are similar to a bed and breakfast in style, but go by the name *Albergo*, *Pensione* or Hotel.)

ROOMS: Agritourism accommodation should not be thought of strictly in terms of the British definition of bed and breakfasts, as in Italy they vary greatly according to each proprietor's interpretation of the concept. The bed and breakfasts in this guide have been described in terms of the criteria used in their selection—warmth of hospitality, historic character, charm of the home, scenery, proximity to sites of touristic interest, and quality of cuisine. Obviously, all of these attributes are not always found in each one. Most of them have an average of six rooms situated either within the family's home or in a separate guesthouse. We have tried to include only those with en-suite bathrooms, as our readers have requested (although for the budget traveler this may not be a priority). Having an extra bed or two added to a room for families with small children is usually not a problem.

APARTMENTS: Since more and more travelers are learning that it is much more advantageous to stay for longer periods in one place (distances are so short between towns within a specific region), apartment-type accommodations with fully-equipped kitchenettes are flourishing. And, in fact, jumping around from one place to another for one or two nights defeats the purpose of a more intimate contact with host families. Apartment accommodation is offered either within the farmhouse along with other units for two to six persons, or as a full house rental for six to ten persons. They are rented by the week from Saturday to Saturday throughout the country, the exception being during the low season. No meals are included unless the bed and breakfast also has a restaurant or makes special arrangements for breakfast. Rates include use of all facilities, unless otherwise indicated, linens, and utilities. There is usually an extra charge for heating and once-a-week cleaning. Average apartments for four persons run $500 weekly, a rate hotels cannot beat.

FOOD

A highlight of the agritourism experience is without a doubt the food. Most travelers would agree that a bad meal is hard to find in Italy, a country world-famous for its culinary skills. In the countryside you'll be sampling the traditional recipes from which Italian cuisine originates. Since, whenever possible, all of the ingredients come directly from the farms where you'll be staying, you'll discover the flavorful difference freshness can make. A peek into the farm kitchen is likely to reveal pasta being rolled and cut the old-fashioned way—by hand. Many country cooks prefer to prepare food using traditional methods, and not rely on machines to speed up the process. Guests are usually welcomed into the kitchen for a look around and actual cooking lessons are becoming very popular.

MEALS OFFERED: Bed and breakfasts often serve a Continental breakfast only, of coffee, tea, fresh breads, and jams. However, many prepare other meals and offer (sometimes require) half- or full-board plans. Half board means that breakfast and dinner are both included in the daily per-person room rate. Full board includes the room and all three meals and is less common, since most guests are out and about during the day, or prefer one lighter meal. Dinner is a hearty three-course meal, often shared at a common table with the host family, and most times includes wine and other beverages. Menus might be set daily, according to the availability of fresh produce, or a limited choice may be given. Some farms have a full-fledged restaurant serving non-guests as well. Travelers who are not necessarily guests at a particular bed and breakfast may take advantage of this opportunity to sample other fare. It is advisable to reserve in advance.

Introduction–About Bed & Breakfasts

ENGLISH

English spoken at each bed and breakfast has been indicated as follows: fluent, very well, well, some, little, or none. We would like to note, however, that this is just an indication, as the person who speaks English may or may not be there during your stay. In any case, it is helpful (not to mention rewarding) to have a few basic Italian phrases on hand. A phrase book or dictionary is indispensable. And when all else fails, the art of communicating with gestures is still very much alive in Italy!

LENGTH OF STAY

Agriturismo is most advantageous for those who have more than the standard one week to travel. Bed-and-breakfast accommodations take longer to reach, for one thing, and **often they are neither set up nor staffed for one-night stays** which increase costs and defeat the purpose. There are numerous exceptions, however, especially in bed and breakfasts near cities, where overnight guests are accepted. It is noted in the description where a minimum stay is required.

WHEN TO VISIT

Since agritourism accommodation is usually in permanent residences, many remain open all year, but most are open only from Easter through November. If you are traveling outside this time, however, it is worth a phone call to find out if the bed and breakfast will accommodate you anyway (at very affordable rates). The best time for agritourism is without a doubt during the spring and fall months, when nature is in its glory. You can enjoy the flowers blossoming in May, the *vendemia*, or grape harvest, at the end of September, the fall foliage in late October, or olive-oil production and truffle hunts in November and December. Southern Italy can be mild and pleasant in the winter, which might be perfect for travelers who like to feel they are the only tourists around. The vast majority of Italians vacation at the same time, during the month of August, Easter weekend, and Christmas, so these time periods are best avoided, if possible.

WHAT TO SEE AND DO

Bed and breakfast proprietors take pride in their farms and great pleasure in answering questions about their agricultural activity. They will often take time to explain and demonstrate procedures such as wine making, olive pressing or cheese production. They are the best source for, and are happy to suggest, restaurants and local itineraries including historic sites, picturesque villages, and cultural activities. Your hosts feel responsible for entertaining their guests and many have added swimming pools or tennis courts if they are not already available in the vicinity. Other activities such as archery, fishing, hiking, and biking are sometimes offered. Horseback riding has made an enormous comeback and farms frequently have their own stables and organize lessons and/or excursions into the countryside.

PLANNING YOUR TRIP

Italian Government Travel Offices (ENIT) can offer general information on various regions and their cultural attractions. They cannot offer specific information on restaurants and accommodations. Offices are located in:

Chicago: Italian Government Travel Office, 401 N. Michigan Ave., Suite 3030, Chicago, IL 60611 USA; tel: (312) 644-0990, fax: (312) 644-3019. (Open 9 am to 1 pm. Mail, fax, or phone only.)

Los Angeles: Italian Government Travel Office, 12400 Wilshire Blvd. Suite 550, Los Angeles, CA 90026, USA; tel: (310) 820-0098, fax: (310) 820-6357.

New York: Italian Government Travel Office, 630 5th Ave., Suite 1565, New York, NY 10111, USA; tel: (212) 245-4822, fax: (212) 586-9249.

Montreal: Italian Government Travel Office, 1 Place Ville Marie, Suite 1914, Montreal, Quebec H3B 3M9, Canada; tel: (514) 866-7667, fax: (514) 392-1429.

London: Italian Government Travel Office, 1 Princes Street, London WIR 8AY, England; tel: (0171) 408-1254, fax: (0171) 493-6695.

Sydney and Auckland: These areas are covered by the Tokyo office—Italian Government Travel Office, Itaria Seifu Kanko Kyoku (ENIT) Lion's Building -1-1-2, Moto Akasaka Minato-Ku, Tokyo 107 Japan; tel: (3) 3478-2051 or 2052, fax: (3) 3479-9356.

RATES

Room rates vary according to size, location, season, and level of service. Rates range from $50 to $200 for a double room with breakfast (indicated as B&B in the following descriptions) and from $35 to $100 per person for room with half board. The majority of the bed and breakfasts selected for this guide have private bathrooms. **Approximate prices for 1996 are indicated in lire and are by no means fixed**. Rates include tax and breakfast unless otherwise indicated, and are **confirmed at time of reservation**. Because of its cost advantages, agritourism is an ideal choice for a family vacation. Children under eight are offered a discount and hosts will almost always add an extra bed for a small charge. There are some wonderful benefits to traveling in the low season (November to March with the exception of holidays) in Italy. The considerable reduction in bed-and-breakfast rates combined with irresistibly low air fares makes it a super-economical vacation. And then, there's the ultimate advantage of not having to fight for space with crowds of other tourists. Italy is all yours!

CREDIT CARDS

Credit cards are rarely accepted, cash being the preferred method of payment. When "plastic payment" is taken, the type of card accepted will be indicated as follows: AX: American Express; MC: Master Card; VS: Visa; or all major.

RESERVATIONS

Whether you plan to stay in several bed and breakfasts or decide to remain for an extended period in just one, **advance reservations are preferred**. Not only do many of the bed and breakfasts have only a few bedrooms available, but also they are usually in private homes which are not prepared to take walk-in traffic. There are several ways to make a reservation:

Fax: Many places to stay (especially in or near cities) have fax numbers. Faxing is a quick way to make a reservation (remember to include your fax number for their response). A reservation request letter in Italian with an English translation is on the following page.

Letter: You can write to the bed and breakfast (allow up to six weeks for an answer because mail to and from Italy is very slow). Make photocopies of the sample reservation-request letter. (Note: In correspondence, be sure to spell out the month.) Frequently a deposit is requested in order to confirm the reservation.

Reservation Service: If you want to pay for the convenience of having the reservations made for you, pre-payments made, vouchers issued, and cars rented, any of the bed and breakfasts in this guide can be booked through **Hidden Treasures of Italy**, a booking service run by the author of this guide, Nicole Franchini. Further information as to the charges and the request form are found following the index, at the back of this book.

Telephone: You can call the bed and breakfast directly. This is very efficient since you will get an immediate response. (The level of English spoken is given in each bed and breakfast description.) To telephone Italy from the United States, dial 011 (the international code), then 39 (Italy's code), then the city code (dropping the 0 outside Italy), and the telephone number. Italy is six hours ahead of New York.

Travel Agent: Travel agents will charge for their services since it is time-consuming to make reservations and most places to stay are too small to pay any commission to compensate for the costs involved.

HOTEL RESERVATION REQUEST LETTER IN ITALIAN

HOTEL NAME & ADDRESS—clearly printed or typed

Vi prego di voler riservare:
I would like to request:

Numero delle camere con bagno o doccia privata _____
Number of rooms with private bath or shower

Numero delle camere senza bagno o doccia _____
Number of rooms without private bath or shower

Data di arrivo _____ Data di partenza _____
Date of arrival *Date of departure*

Vi prego inoltre de fornirmi le seguenti informazioni:
Please let me know as soon as possible the following:

Potete riservare le camere richieste? Si / No
Can you reserve the space requested? *Yes / No*

I pasti sono compresi nel prezzo? Si / No
Are meals included in your rate? *Yes / No*

E necessario un deposito? Si / No
Do you need a deposit? *Yes / No*

Prezzo giornaliero _____
Price per night

Quanto e necessario come deposito? _____
How much deposit do you need?

Ringraziando anticipatamente, porgo distinti saluti,
Thanking you in advance, I send my best regards,

YOUR NAME & ADDRESS—clearly printed or typed

FINDING YOUR BED AND BREAKFAST

At the back of the book is a key map of the whole of Italy plus thirteen regional maps showing each recommended hotel's location. The pertinent regional map number is given at the right on the *top line* of each hotel's description. To make it easier for you, we have divided each location map into a grid of four parts, a, b, c, and d, as indicated on each map's key. Directions to help you find your destination are given after each bed and breakfast description. However, they are only a small clue, as it would be impossible to find the space to give more details, and to know from which direction the traveler is arriving. The beauty of many of these lodgings is that they are off the beaten track, but that characteristic may also make them very tricky to find. If you get lost, a common occurrence, first keep your sense of humor, then call the proprietors and/or ask locals at bars or gas stations for directions. As previously mentioned, detailed maps for the area in which you will be traveling are essential. It is important to know that addresses in the countryside often have no specific street name. A common address consists of the farm name, sometimes a *localita* (an unincorporated area, or vicinity, frequently not found on a map) and the town name followed by the province abbreviated in parentheses. (The bed and breakfast is not necessarily in that town, but it serves as a post office reference.) The localita can also be the name of the road where the bed and breakfast is located, to make things more confusing. We state the localita as the third line of the bed and breakfast information.

TRANSFERS INTO CITIES: Travelers from abroad normally arrive by plane in Milan, Rome, or Venice and pick up their rental car at the airport. However, if your first destination is the city and you plan on picking up your car after your stay, approximate transfer rates are as follows:

MILAN

From Malpensa to city by taxi (70 min)	Lire 125,000
From Malpensa to city by bus	Lire 18,000

From Linate to city by taxi (20 min)	Lire 45,000
From Linate to city by bus	Lire 2,500
ROME	
From Da Vinci to city by train (1 hour)	Lire 15,000
From Da Vinci to city by taxi (45 min)	Lire 80,000
VENICE	
From airport to city by waterbus (1 hour)	Lire 15,000
From station to city by waterbus (15 min)	Lire 4,000
From station to city by private watertaxi	Lire 85,000

REGIONAL FARM NAMES

The following names for farms, seen throughout this guide, vary from area to area.

azienda agricola—a general term meaning farm, not necessarily offering hospitality

borgo—a small stone-walled village, usually of medieval origins

casale, casolare—variations of farmhouse, deriving from "casa"

cascina and ca'—farmhouse in Piedmont, Lombardy, and Veneto

fattoria—typically a farm in Tuscany or Umbria

hof and maso—terms meaning house and farm in the northern mountain areas

locanda—historically a restaurant with rooms for travelers passing through on horseback

masseria—fortified farms in Apulia, Sicily

podere—land surrounding a farmhouse

poggio—literally describes the farm's position on a flat hilltop

tenuta—estate

torre—tower

trattoria—a simple, family-run restaurant in cities and the countryside

villa and castello—usually former home of nobility and more elaborate in services

About Italy

The following pointers are given in alphabetical order, not in order of importance.

BANKS

Banking hours are Monday through Friday from 8:30 am to 1:30 pm and 3 to 4 pm. *Cambio* signs outside and inside a bank indicate that it will exchange traveler's checks or give you cash from certain credit cards. Also privately-run exchange offices are available in cities with more convenient hours and comparable rates.

DRIVING

A car is a must for this type of travel—most bed and breakfasts are inaccessible by any other means of transportation. A car gives the traveler a great deal of independence (public transportation is frequently on strike in Italy), while providing the ideal means to explore the countryside thoroughly. It is best to reserve a vehicle and pre-pay by credit card before your departure to insure the best rates possible.

DRIVER'S LICENSE: An International Driver's Permit is not necessary for renting a car as a tourist: a foreign driver's license is valid for driving throughout Italy, which is not quite the "vehicular-free-for-all" you may have heard about, at least not outside big cities (particularly Rome, Florence, and Milan). When visiting Rome, it's advisable to do so at the beginning or end of your trip, before you pick up or after you drop off your car, and, by all means, avoid driving within the city. Italians have a different relationship with the basic rules of the road: common maneuvers include running stop lights and stop signs, triple-parking, driving at 100 mph on the highways, passing on the right, and backing up at missed highway exits. But once out of the city, you will find it relatively easy to reach your destination. Road directions are quite good in Italy and people are very willing to help.

DISTANCES: Distances are indicated in kilometers (one kilometer equals 0.621 mile), calculated roughly into miles by cutting the kilometer distance in half. Distances between towns are also indicated in orange alongside the roads on the Touring Club Italiano maps. Italy is a compact country and distances are relatively short, yet you will be amazed at how dramatically the scenery can change in an hour's drive.

GASOLINE: Gas prices in Italy are the highest in Europe, and Americans often suspect a mistake when their first fill-up comes to between $45 and $80 (most of it in taxes). Some stations now accept Visa credit cards, and the ERG stations accept American Express. Besides the AGIP stations on the autostrade, which are almost always open, gas stations observe the same hours as merchants, closing in the afternoon from 12:30 to 4 and in the evening at 7:30. Be careful not to get caught running on empty in the afternoon! Many stations have a self-service pump that operates on off-hours and accepts only 10,000-lire bills.

MAPS: An above-average map of Italy is absolutely essential for this type of travel. The Touring Club Italiano maps, in an easy-to-read three-volume format divided into North, Central, and South, is a superior selection. Even the smallest town or, better, *localita* is indicated in the extensive index. In addition, places of particular interest are underlined or boxed in green, as are exceptionally scenic roads. Another fine choice are the Rand McNally *Hallwag* maps. Depending upon your itinerary, you need either their *Northern Italy* or *Southern Italy* map, or both (the whole-country map isn't specific enough). Each comes with a small index booklet to help you locate the towns.

ROADS: Names of roads in Italy are as follows:

Autostrada: a large, fast (and most direct) two- or three-lane tollway, marked by green signs bearing an "A" followed by the autostrada number. As you enter you receive a ticket from an automatic machine by pushing a red button. Payment is made at your exit point. If you lose your card, you will have to pay the equivalent amount of the distance from the beginning of the autostrada to your exit.

Superstrada: a one- or two-lane freeway between secondary cities marked by blue signs and given a number. Speed limit: 110 kph.

Strada Statale: a small one-lane road marked with S.S. followed by the road number. Speed limit: 90 kph.

Raccordo or *Tangenziale*: a ring road around main cities, connecting to an autostrada and city centers.

ROAD SIGNS: Yellow signs are for tourists and indicate a site of historical or cultural interest, hotels, and restaurants. Black-and-yellow signs indicate the name and location of private companies and industries.

TOLLS: Tolls on Italian autostrade are quite steep, ranging from $15 to $20 for a three-hour stretch, but offering the fastest and most direct way to travel between cities. Fortunately for the agritourist, tollways are rarely necessary. However, if it suits your needs, a *Viacard*, or magnetic reusable card for tolls, is available in all tollway gas stations for 50,000 or 90,000 lire (the lines for the automatic machines taking these cards are always shortest).

HOLIDAYS

It is very important to know Italian holidays because most museums, shops, and offices are closed. National holidays are listed below:

New Year's Day (January 1)
Epiphany (January 6)
Easter (and the following Monday)
Liberation Day (April 25)
Labor Day (May 1)

Assumption Day (August 15)
All Saints' Day (November 1)
Christmas (December 25)
Santo Stefano (December 26)

In addition to the national holidays, each town also has its own special holiday to honor its patron saint. Some of the major ones are listed below:

Bologna—St. Petronio (October 4)
Florence—St. John the Baptist (June 24)
Milan—St. Ambrose (December 7)

Palermo—Santa Rosalia (July 15)
Rome—St. Peter (June 29)
Venice—St. Mark (April 25)

The Vatican in Rome has its own schedule. The museums are closed every Sunday, except the last Sunday of each month when admission is free.

PROVINCES

Italy is divided into provinces which are indicated in addresses and on license plates (although being phased out) in abbreviated form as follows:

AL Alessandria	AN Ancona	AR Arezzo	AP Ascoli Picino
AT Asti	BA Bari	BL Belluno	BG Bergamo
BO Bologna	BZ Bolzano	BS Brescia	BR Brindisi
CZ Catanzaro	CO Como	FI Firenze	FO Forli
GE Genova	GO Gorizia	GR Grosseto	LU Lucca
MN Mantova	MI Milano	MO Modena	NA Napoli
NO Novara	PD Padova	PR Parma	PV Pavia
PG Perugia	PS Pesaro	PI Pisa	PT Pistoia
PZ Potenza	RA Ravenna	SA Salerno	SV Savona
SI Siena	TA Taranto	TR Terni	TO Torino
TN Trento	TV Treviso	VE Venezia	VC Vercelli
VR Verona	VI Vicenza	VT Viterbo	

REGIONS

For reference, the 20 regions of Italy from north to south, with their capital cities in parentheses, are as follows:

NORTH—Valle d'Aosta (Aosta), Liguria (Genova), Piedmont (Torino), Friuli Venezia Giulia (Trieste), Trentino-Alto Adige (Trento & Bolzano), Lombardy (Milan), Veneto (Venice), and Emilia-Romagna (Bologna).

CENTRAL—Tuscany (Florence), Umbria (Perugia), Marches (Ancona), Lazio (Rome), Abruzzo (L'Aquila), and Molise (Campobasso).

SOUTH—Campania (Naples), Apulia (Bari), Calabria (Cantazaro), Basilicata (Potenza), Sicily (Palermo), and Sardinia (Caliari).

SAFETY

If certain precautions are taken, most unfortunate incidents can be avoided. It is extremely helpful to keep copies of passports, tickets, and contents of your wallet in your hotel room in case you need them. Pickpocketing most commonly occurs in cities on buses, train stations, crowded streets, or from passing motorbikes. WARNING: At tollway gas stations and snack bars, **always** lock your car and beware of gypsies and vendors who try to sell you stolen merchandise. This practice is most prevalent south of Rome. In general, **never** leave valuables or even luggage in the car. Also, **never** set down luggage even for a minute in train stations.

SHOPPING

Italy is a shopper's paradise. Not only are the stores brimming with tempting merchandise, but the displays are works of art, from the tiniest fruit market to the most chic boutique. Each region seems to specialize in something: in Venice hand-blown glass and handmade lace are popular; Milan is famous for its clothing and silk; Florence is a center for leather goods and gold jewelry; Rome is a fashion hub, where you can stroll the pedestrian shopping streets and browse in some of the world's most elegant shops boasting the latest designer creations. Religious items are also plentiful in Rome, particularly near St. Peter's Cathedral. Naples and the surrounding area (Capri, Ravello, and Positano) offer delightful coral jewelry and also a wonderful selection of ceramics. You will be enticed by the variety of products sold at the farms such as wines, virgin olive oil, jams and honeys, cheese, and salami, along with local artisans' handicrafts. NOTE: For reasons of financial control and the tax evasion problems in Italy, the law states that clients **must** leave commercial establishments with an official receipt in hand, in order to avoid fines.

For purchases over 300,000 lire an immediate cash refund of the tax amount is offered by the Italian government. Goods must be purchased at an affiliated retail outlet with the "tax-free for tourists" sign. Ask for the store receipt **plus** the tax-free shopping receipt. At the airport go first to the customs office where they will examine the items purchased and stamp both receipts, and then to the "tax-free cash refund" point after passport control.

US customs allows US residents to bring in $400-worth of foreign goods duty-free, after which a straight 10% of the amount above $400 is levied. Two bottles of liquor are allowed. The import of fresh cheese or meat is strictly restricted unless it is vacuum-packed.

TELEPHONES

The Italian phone company (the infamous SIP, now called TELECOMM) has been an object of ridicule, a source of frustration and a subject of heated conversation since its inception; and rightfully so. Over half of the phone calls initiated are never completed. Although more modern systems are being installed, it remains one of most archaic, inefficient, and costly communication systems in the developed world, though touch-tone phones are now found in parts of some cities. To make matters at least not any worse, keep the following in mind (and be prepared to "try, try again"): to make a call within Italy, always dial "0" before the area code; from outside Italy, the "0" is eliminated. Telephone numbers can have from four to eight digits so don't be afraid of missing numbers. Cellular phone numbers begin with 0330, 0336, or 0337.

Dial 113 for emergencies of all kinds—24-hour service nationwide.

Dial 116 for Automobile Club for urgent breakdown assistance on the road.

Remember that no warning is given when the time you've paid for is about to expire (the line just goes dead), so put in plenty of change. Unused coins will be refunded. There are several types of phones (in various stages of modernization) in Italy:

Gray phones (slowly being phased out) are best for local calls. These take *gettoni,* or tokens, which are available at bars and tobacco stores for 200 lire.

Regular rotary phones in bars, restaurants, and many bed and breakfasts, which you can use *a scatti,* meaning you can pay the proprietor after the call is completed.

Bright orange pay phones which accept 500-, 200-, and 100-lire coins as well as *gettoni.* Bright orange pay phones as above with attached apparatus permitting insertion of a *scheda telefonica,* or reusable magnetic card worth 5,000 or 10,000 lire.

NOTE: Due to the ongoing modernization process of telephone lines, phone numbers are constantly being changed, making it sometimes very difficult to contact lodgings (many times they are not listed under the lodging's name). A recording (in Italian) plays for only two months indicating the new number. If you are calling from the United States and your Italian is not up to par, we suggest you ask the overseas operator to contact the Italian operator for translation and assistance.

To call the United States from Italy, matters have been eased by the ongoing installation of the Country Direct System, whereby with one 200-lire coin you can reach an American operator by dialing either 172-1011 for AT&T or 172-1022 for MCI. Be patient and wait the one to two minutes before a recording or US operator comes through. Either a collect call or a credit-card call can then be placed. If you discover this system doesn't work from some smaller towns, dial 170 to place a collect call, or, in some cities, try dialing direct (from a *scatti* phone), using the international code 001 + area code + number.

TIPPING

Hotels: a service charge is included in the daily rate. A token tip for the chambermaid for longer stays is common practice. Restaurants: 15% is included in the bill's total. It is customary, however, to leave from 3,000–8,000 lire for the waiter, depending on service. Taxis: 10%.

TRAIN TRAVEL

Although a car is an absolute necessity to reach most bed and breakfasts, it is often convenient and time-saving to leave the car and take a train for day trips into the city. NOTE: A new policy has just been established by the country's national train network—your ticket must be stamped with the time and date **before** you board the train, otherwise you will be issued a 40,000 lire fine. Tickets are stamped at small and not very obvious yellow machines near the exits to the tracks. Unstamped tickets may be reimbursed with a 30% penalty. It is strongly advised that you purchase your ticket (including seat reservation) in advance through a local travel agency when you arrive in order to avoid long lines at the station. The IC and EC trains to major cities are the most efficient.

We wish you the best in your travels to Italy and always welcome your comments and suggestions. *Buon Viaggio!*

Descriptions of Places to Stay

In the heart of the wine valley of Piedmont, just outside and above the town of Alba, is the stately, cream-colored villa belonging to Giuliana Pionzo and her husband—Cascina Reine's gracious hosts. Besides a lovely flower garden and above-ground pool (open only in July and August), the large home has a terra-cotta roof, a lovely arcaded patio, and a fabulous view over Alba's rooftops and the surrounding countryside. Wicker chairs with plump floral cushions invite guests to relax on the patio, where at sunset they may also enjoy a refreshing mint drink with the *simpatico* hosts. Accommodation is offered within the ivy-covered main house, each room finely decorated with antiques, paintings, and the family's personal objects A suite consisting of two bedrooms, bath, and large terrace is ideal for a family of four. Other newer rooms have been recently added in the wing adjoining the villa, one with its own terrace and kitchenette. Breakfast is served either outside on the patio overlooking the vineyards and orchards, or inside in the pristine dining room with vaulted ceilings. Alba has some of the finest restaurants in Italy and is also famous for its wines and annual truffle festival. *Directions:* From Alba follow signs for Altavilla and Mango. Watch for a small sign on the left before the large wrought-iron gates of the inn.

CASCINA REINE
Hostess: Giuliana Pionzo
Localita: Altavilla 9
Alba (CN) 12051, Italy
Tel: (0173) 440112
9 rooms, 7 with private bathrooms
Lire 110,000–130,000 double B&B
Breakfast only (dinner upon request)
Open all year
Very little English spoken
Region: Piedmont

Seven kilometers from historic Bergamo and within easy reach of beautiful Lakes Como, Iseo, and Garda is the home of the region's agritourist president, Gianantonio Ardizzone. On Gianantonio's property, next to the recently constructed residence where he and his family live, is a sprawling 15th-century farmhouse and barn complex of the type known in Lombardy as a *cascina.* Installed within the cascina are three guest apartments, each including a bedroom, bathroom, and kitchen. The apartments are furnished modestly but comfortably, with a decidedly rustic ambiance within and without. The cascina could perhaps use a coat of paint, but it is nestled in pretty surroundings, looking onto the small town of Nese, and backing onto the green hills where Gianantonio keeps his well tended riding horses. No meals are served here, but a nearby trattoria adequately appeases the appetite, or you may want to do some shopping before you arrive and come ready to prepare your own meals. The Grumello offers self-sufficient, conveniently located accommodation and a good value. Your hosts are exceptionally helpful and sincerely warm. *Directions:* Exit from A4 autostrada at Bergamo and follow signs for Valli di Bergamo, Valle Seriana. Exit at Alzano after 6 kilometers and follow hospital signs; go straight on for Nese and turn left on Via Grumello.

CASCINA GRUMELLO
Hosts: Gianantonio Ardizzone family
Localita: Fraz. Nese
Alzano Lombardo (BG) 24022, Italy
Tel: (035) 510060 Fax: (035) 711020
3 apartments
Lire 35,000 per person (heating/cleaning extra)
No meals served
Open all year
Credit cards: VS
Some English spoken
Region: Lombardy

For something very different from the more hotel-like ambiance of the Locanda of Ansedonia, the Grazia farm next door is an excellent alternative. Gracious and warm hostess, Signora Maria Grazia, divides her time between Rome and the 300-acre property she inherited from her grandfather. The dramatic cypress-lined driveway takes you away from the busy Aurelia road up to the expansive salmon-hued edifice with its arched loggia. The hosts' home, office, three guest apartments, farmhands' quarters, and horse stalls are all housed within the complex which is encased by superb country and sea views in all directions. From here one can enjoy touring Etruscan territory: Tuscania, Tarquinia, Sovana, Sorano, and the nearby ruins of Cosa, or stay seaside on the beaches of Feniglia on the promontory of Argentario. Comfortable accommodations pleasantly decorated with homey touches are offered within any of three apartments for two to six persons including living area and kitchen. Our favorite is the two-bedroom apartment on the second floor capturing the front view to the sea through the trees. Maria Grazia can suggest a number of local restaurants specializing in seafood. Altogether a delightful combination. *Directions*: Take the coastal Aurelia road from Rome and after the Ansedonia exit turn right into an unmarked driveway immediately after the Pitorsino restaurant.

GRAZIA **NEW**
Hosts: Maria Grazia Cantore family
Via Aurelia, km 140.1
Orbetello Scalo (GR) 58016, Italy
Tel: (0564) 881182 or (06) 483945
3 apartments
Lire 40,000 per person daily
3-day minimum stay
No meals served
Open all year
English spoken well
Region: Tuscany

Anna and Gabriele's small inn just outside the seaside resort of Argentario, a favorite of Romans, is one of the few that offers moderately priced and attractive accommodations. Only a short ride from the quaint port towns of Porto Ercole and Porto Santo Stefano, the island of Giglio, within hailing distance of a panoramic coastal drive rivaling that of Amalfi, and only 1½ hour's drive from Fiumicino airport, La Locanda guarantees a relaxing stay in an intimate setting. The inn's 12 air-conditioned guestrooms all include bathrooms, and are simply and newly appointed. Rooms off the garden are recommended as the others face the busy main Aurelia road. All meals, featuring innovative southern Tuscan cuisine based on meat and fresh fish, are served in the public restaurant, either in the inside dining room with fireplace for the cooler months, or the glassed-in summer dining room overlooking a lush garden, giving the illusion of being deep in the countryside. *Directions:* Take the Aurelia highway north from Rome. After the turnoff for Ansedonia before Orbetello, turn right at the inn sign. From Florence: take the superstrada to Grosseto, then the Aurelia road towards Rome, turning off after Orbetello at Ansedonia. Follow signs back to the inn on the opposite side.

LA LOCANDA DI ANSEDONIA
Hosts: Anna Maria Bonsanti & Gabriele Rum
Via Aurelia Sud, km 140.5
Orbetello (GR) 58015, Italy
Tel: (0564) 881317 Fax: (0564) 881727
12 rooms with private bathrooms
Lire 100,000–160,000 double B&B
All meals served
Open all year
Credit cards: AX, VS
Very little English spoken
Region: Tuscany

Few visitors to the spiritual city of Assisi are aware that the Subasio mountains flanking it feature some of the most breathtaking scenery in the country. Nestled there is a cluster of stone houses known as Le Silve, a village which served as a haven for 10th-century pilgrims traveling from the Adriatic coast to Rome. Carrying on that tradition of offering home-cooked meals and impeccable hospitality, Signora Taddia has recreated an ambiance of utter tranquillity, while adding her own touch of elegance. The guestrooms are tastefully furnished with simple antiques which blend harmoniously with the preserved medieval architecture. The main house contains 15 bedrooms with private bathrooms, and panoramic views, reception, and a living room with fireplace. The auxiliary house has a beamed dining room, billiard and card rooms. This bed and breakfast features many of the amenities of a luxury hotel, including swimming pool, tennis, and horseback riding. *Directions:* From Assisi go in the direction of Gualdo Tadino. One passes close to and should not miss the Eremo (site of St. Francis's retreat). Take the winding uphill road at the sign for Armenzano and follow it for 15 kilometers. The hotel is after Armenzano village and is well marked.

LE SILVE DI ARMENZANO
Hostess: Daniela Taddia
Localita: Armenzano
Assisi (PG) 06081, Italy
Tel: (075) 8019000 Fax: (075) 8019005
15 rooms with private bathrooms, 4 suites,
7 apartments
Lire 260,000–420,000 double B&B
Open March to November
Credit cards: all major
Fluent English spoken
Region: Umbria

The delightful Malvarina farm has all the ingredients for the perfect bed and breakfast: charming country-style accommodations, excellent local cuisine, a warm and congenial host family, and an ideal location. Just outside town, yet immersed in lush green vegetation at the foot of the Subasio mountains, the property is comprised of the 15th-century stone farmhouse where the family lives and four independent cottages (converted barn and stalls) divided into bedrooms and suites with en-suite bathrooms, plus three apartments with kitchenettes for two to four persons. *Casa Angelo* holds several bedrooms plus a sweet breakfast room with a corner fireplace and cupboards filled with colorful *Deruta* ceramics. Great care has obviously been taken in the decor of rooms, using Maria's family's heirloom furniture. The old wine cellar has been cleverly converted into a cool and spacious taverna dining room with long wooden tables for dining *en famille*. A collection of antique farm tools and brass pots cover walls near the enormous fireplace. Horses are available for trekking into the scenic national park just beyond the house. *Directions:* Exit at Capodacqua from the Perugia-Spello route 75. Turn right then left on Via Massera (Radio Subasio sign) and follow the road up to Malvarina.

MALVARINA
Hosts: Claudio & Luciano Fabrizi
Localita: Malvarina 32
Assisi (PG) 06080, Italy
Tel & fax: (075) 8064280
10 rooms with private bathrooms, 3 apartments
Lire 110,000 double B&B (3-day minimum stay)
*　90,000 per person half board*
Breakfast and dinner served
Open all year
Credit cards: all major
Some English spoken
Region: Umbria

Fabrizio and Bianca, the Milanese hosts originally from this part of Umbria, restored their inherited La Fornace farmhouse, situated in the very desirable touring location of Assisi, with their guests' comfort foremost in mind. With careful attention to detail, four comfortable apartments were fashioned within the three stone houses, each with one or two bedrooms, bathroom, fully equipped kitchenette, and eating area. Interesting decorating touches such as parts of antique iron gates hung over beds, terra-cotta and white ceramic tiles in the immaculate bathrooms, and antique armoires give the accommodations a polished country flavor. *Le Pannocchie*, the largest of the four, includes a corner fireplace, while *Papaveri*, on the second floor, looks out over the flat cornfields up to magnificent Assisi and the Subasio mountains beyond. The Cascioli family takes care of guests' needs when the owners are not in residence and assures that each room is stocked with breakfast fixings each morning. This is an excellent base from which to visit such Umbrian marvels as Perugia, Spoleto, Todi, and Gubbio. A swimming pool has just been completed. *Directions:* From Perugia-Spoleto highway 75, exit at Ospedalicchio on route 147, turn left for Tordibetto after the bridge, then right for Assisi and follow signs for La Fornace.

PODERE LA FORNACE
Hosts: Bianca & Fabrizio Feliciani
Via Ombrosa 3
Tordibetto di Assisi (PG) 06081, Italy
Tel & fax: (075) 8019537 or (0330) 282154
4 apartments
Lire 105,000–250,000 daily per apartment
3-day minimum stay
Breakfast included with weekly stays
Open all year
English spoken well (hosts)
Region: Umbria

Situated just a few kilometers from the Gulf of Taranto, and strategically based between the cities of Gallipoli, Taranto, and Lecce, is the villa of Giacinto Mannarini, a sprawling, whitewashed modern inn built on the original site of the Mudonato castle. Signor Mannarini offers warm hospitality in ten guestrooms in the main house, which are reached through separate entrances off an arcaded breezeway. Spotless rooms are furnished with rustic reproductions in dark wood. Triple rooms now have air conditioning installed. An apartment for four people includes a living room but no kitchen facilities. The property covers 100 acres of forest and olive groves and boasts a lovely swimming pool with a kitchen serving meals on the poolside patio. The fine cuisine (cited in the Veronelli restaurant guide) is prepared from the freshest available produce and features homemade pastas (the local *orecchiette*, or ear pasta) and desserts. Vegetarian dishes are also available, as is a full American breakfast. Signor Giacinto is a delightful host and is knowledgeable on his native Apulia. *Directions:* From Taranto take route 7 through Manduria and Avetrana. Three kilometers out of town toward Salice turn left at the sign for Mudonato.

BOSCO DI MUDONATO
Host: Giacinto Mannarini
Via per Salice-Casella Postale 2
Avetrana (TA) 74020, Italy
Tel & fax: (099) 8704597
10 rooms with private bathrooms
Lire 160,000 double B&B (2-day minimum)
 105,000 per person half board
Advance reservation required
All meals served
Open all year
English spoken well
Region: Apulia

Tucked away in the hills of Montalbano, 38 kilometers from Florence, is the lovely Bacchereto farm owned by the Bencini Tesi family. The farm comprises several historic buildings, the main house being where the family resides and breakfast is served. At a long table with visible signs of hundreds of years of use, guests are served fresh breads and homemade jams and honey. The best rooms are in the *Palazzina,* an 18th-century garden and villa with seven double rooms (three with private bath) tastefully furnished with family antiques. Well worn terra-cotta floors and beamed ceilings add to the historic atmosphere, and the kitchen and living room are at guests' disposal. The Palazzina can also be rented out weekly as a full house, as can four houses for two to nine persons scattered about the large estate. The family owns an exceptional restaurant, *La Cantina di Toia* (cited in the Veronelli guide), in town within a building once home to Leonardo da Vinci's grandmother! Other more modest rooms are available upstairs. Maitre d' Gennaro attends meticulously to patrons, and offers an excellent selection of wines including the estate's own chianti *Carmignano of Bacchereto. Directions:* From Florence (25 kilometers) take autostrada A1 to the Firenze Nord/Prato exit. Follow signs for Poggio a Caiano, Saeno, then to Bacchereto.

FATTORIA DI BACCHERETO
Hosts: Carlo Bencini Tesi family
Via Fontemorana 179
Bacchereto Carmignano (FI) 50040, Italy
Tel & fax: (055) 8717191
11 rooms, 4 with private bathrooms
5 apartments
Lire 80,000–154,000 double B&B
 Lire 750,000–1,800,000 weekly for apts
Trattoria on premises
Open all year
English spoken well
Region: Tuscany

After many years of traveling to Italy at any free opportunity, Jennie and Alan left England to move to Tuscany and fell in love immediately with Villa Mimosa, a 16th-century home with front courtyard and now-extinct olive oil press on the ground floor. Alan got to work right away with restoring and transforming the upstairs into guest quarters, creating three sweet bedrooms, each with a different scheme. He added small, but very practical bathrooms in each room. Two cozy sitting rooms upstairs are reserved for guests and decorated with the Pratts' antiques shipped over from home, grand piano, and library books. Jennie and Alan's idea with offering few rooms was to share their passion for this part of the country known as Lunigiana (very near the Cinque Terre coastal area) and give their guests lots of personal attention, while making them feel right at home. Guests are treated to breakfast on the terrace overlooking the vegetable garden and Apennine mountains. While Alan continues working on his many renovation projects, Jennie concentrates on producing delightful cuisine based on fresh vegetables. A perfect stopover. *Directions:* Exit from the A15 autostrada (Parma-La Spezia) at Pontremoli from the north or Aulla from the south and head towards Villafranca, then Bagnone. Enter town through the gateway and turn left at Via N Quartieri. Go uphill for 3 kilometers and Villa Mimosa is on the left before the church.

VILLA MIMOSA   **NEW**
Hosts: Jennie & Alan Pratt
Localita: Corlaga
Bagnone (MS) 52401, Italy
Tel: (0187) 427022
3 bedrooms with private bathrooms
Lire 90,000 double B&B
Breakfast, dinner upon request
Open all year
English spoken fluently
Region: Tuscany

In the heart of the Veneto region, south of Vicenza, lies the Castello winery and estate, a handsome 15th-century villa watching proudly over the sweet town of Barbarano Vicentino and the home of the Marinoni family for the past century. Signora Elda, along with her two young sons, carries on the tradition. The large walled courtyard with manicured Renaissance garden is bordered by the family's home, the guesthouse (originally farmer's quarters), and converted barn, where concerts and banquets are organized. A lovely courtyard overlooks the family's expansive vineyards from which fine red wines are produced. The independent guesthouse overlooking the garden can be rented out as one house or divided into two apartments. The first floor includes a triple bedroom, bathroom, living room, and eat-in kitchen while the second has three doubles, two bathrooms, and a kitchen—all decorated very simply but pleasantly with the family's furnishings. An extra charge is made for heating. It's an easy drive to Padua and Venice where you may opt to leave your car and take the train. *Directions:* Exit from the A4 at Vicenza Est towards Noventa Vicentino, then Barbarano Vicentino. Follow signs to Castello (20 kilometers).

IL CASTELLO
Hosts: Elda Marinoni family
Via Castello 6
Barbarano Vicentino (VI) 36021, Italy
Tel: (0444) 886055
2 apartments
Lire 60,000 double
No meals served
3-day minimum stay, 1 week July and August
Open all year
English spoken well
Region: Veneto

La Casa Sola is just as its name describes—a house standing alone on a hilltop surrounded by bucolic countryside. The proprietors, a noble Genovese family, frequent their lovely 400-acre vineyard property during weekends and holidays, leaving the daily management in the capable hands of the local Regoli family. There are six large guest apartments within a rose-covered stone farmhouse just down the road from the main villa. Apartment number 3 is the loveliest. Installed on two floors, comprised of a living room with fireplace, kitchen, two bedrooms, and two baths, the apartment is furnished in style with refined country antiques. Botanical prints hung with bows, eyelet curtains, fresh flowers, and a bottle of wine are welcoming touches. Another very similar apartment (number 5), for up to eight people, has three bedrooms and magnificent views. The other apartments are smaller and simpler, but each opens onto a private garden. An inviting cypress-edged swimming pool overlooks the valley. The Casa Sola requires a minimum week's stay, and provides an ideal touring base in a tranquil, romantic setting. *Directions:* Exit at San Donato off the Firenze-Siena superstrada. One kilometer after San Donato at the church, turn right onto a dirt road at the sign for Cortine/Casa Sola, and follow it for 7 kilometers.

FATTORIA CASA SOLA
Hosts: Count Gambaro family
Localita: Cortine
Barberino Val d'Elsa (FI) 50021, Italy
Tel: (055) 8075028 Fax: (055) 8059194
6 apartments
Lire 750,000–2,300,000 weekly
  according to apartment size and season
Breakfast and dinner served upon request
Open all year
English spoken well (hosts)
Region: Tuscany

Just off the main road midway between Siena and Florence sits the square stone farmhouse with cupola owned and operated by Gianni and Cristina, a young couple from Milan. The Paretaio appeals particularly to visitors with a passion for horseback riding, for the de Marchis offer everything from basic riding lessons to dressage training, and day outings through the gorgeous surrounding countryside. In fact, the Paretaio is recognized as one of the top riding "ranches" in Tuscany. Next to the saddle room on the first floor is a rustic and warm living room with country antiques and comfy sofas, enhanced by a vaulted brick ceiling and worn terra-cotta floors. Upstairs, the main gathering area is the dining room which features a massive fireplace and a seemingly endless wooden table. Access to the six bedrooms is from this room, and each is stylishly decorated with touches such as dried flowers, white lace curtains, and, of course, equestrian prints. Although riding is the main activity here, the Paretaio organizes courses in Italian and is an excellent base for touring the heart of Tuscany. A new swimming pool is a refreshing addition. *Directions:* Heading south from Barberino (2 kilometers), Paretaio is just off the road at the second right-hand turnoff for San Filippo.

IL PARETAIO
Hosts: Cristina & Giovanni de Marchi
Localita: San Filippo
Barberino Val d'Elsa (FI) 50021, Italy
Tel: (055) 8059218 Fax: (055) 8059231
6 rooms with private bathrooms
Lire 120,000–150,000 double B&B
 95,000–120,000 per person half board
Open all year
English spoken well
Region: Tuscany

La Chiara farm, dating back to 1600 and covering 45 hectares of woods, vineyards, and olive groves, is conveniently located between Siena and Florence in the heart of Chianti, yet affords a feeling of escape. Eleven bedrooms, five with private baths, are dispersed throughout the main villa, which also contains a large living room, kitchen, and dining room where the mostly farm-fresh vegetarian meals using produce from the organic gardens are served. The common rooms and high-ceilinged bedrooms are very modestly furnished with worn country furniture, but are spacious and airy, offering scenic views over the serene countryside. Extra beds can easily be added to rooms, making the Chiara an ideal and economical choice for families traveling with children. The lemon greenhouse and another barn structure have recently been restructured into two apartments. Headed by young and extremely personable Gaia and her husband, the farm is abuzz when groups come for special lectures and courses on art and psychology. There is a small swimming pool not far from the house and horses are available for trekking. *Directions:* Exit at San Donato from the Firenze-Siena highway and after passing San Donato, turn right for Cortine/Casa Sola. Continue to Prumiano (approximately 7 kilometers).

LA CHIARA DI PRUMIANO
Hosts: Gaia Mezzadri & Egidio Pastori
Strada di Cortine 12
Localita: Prumiano
Barberino Val d'Elsa (FI) 50021, Italy
Tel: (055) 8075583 Fax: (055) 8075678
11 rooms, 5 with private bathrooms
2 apartments
Lire 100,000 double B&B
All meals served
Closed January
English spoken well
Region: Tuscany

When the Caccetta family from Rome, along with two other families, purchased the 250-acre property 20 years ago, they were true pioneers in the agritourism field. After many years of bringing back life to both the land and 16th-century hunting lodge, today they have a self-sufficient farm producing Chianti, white and rosé wines, grappa, and olive oil. Spacious guestrooms are divided between the main house, with two suites and three bedrooms, and an adjacent recently restored house. All are decorated with care and attention to detail using lovely family antiques which blend in perfectly with the overall ambiance. The very cozy common rooms downstairs include a living room with fireplace and stone walls, card room, small bar area, and dining rooms where breakfast and dinner are served. A forest-green tartan carpet covers floors and family photos and paintings adorn walls. During the warmer months, meals are served outside under the pergola overlooking deep woods. For those who prefer to stay put, a swimming pool, grass tennis courts, hiking trails, and horseback riding are all available. *Directions*: From the Siena-Florence highway, exit at San Donato and follow the road for Tavarnelle, then Barberino and turn right at the sign for La Spinosa. Take the dirt road to the very end.

LA SPINOSA   **NEW**
Hosts: Paolo Caccetta & Danila Maneri
Via Le Masse 8
Barberino Val d'Elsa (FI) 50021, Italy
Tel & fax: (055) 8075413
5 rooms, 4 suites with private bathrooms
Lire 220,000–260,000 double B&B
* 140,000–160,000 per person half board*
2-day minimum stay
Breakfast and dinner served
Open all year
English spoken very well
Region: Tuscany

The Dreikirchen is situated up in the Dolomite foothills with an enchanting view over a lush green valley and distant snowcapped mountain peaks. The young and energetic Wodenegg family works diligently at making guests feel at home in their lovely residence and running the restaurant which serves typical local meals to non-guest patrons as well since it shares the site of a unique historical monument—*Le Tre Chiese*, three curious, attached, miniature medieval churches. The inn is reachable either by taxi or on foot. An exhilarating half-hour hike takes you up to the typical mountain-style chalet with wood balconies in front. The most charming rooms are those in the older section, entirely wood-paneled, with fluffy comforters and old-fashioned washbasins. The rambling house has several common areas for guests as well as a swimming pool. This is truly an incredible spot, near Siusi Alps and Val Gardena where some of the best climbing in Europe can be found. *Directions:* Exit from the Bolzano-Brennero autostrada at Klausen and take the road south to Ponte Gardena and through Barbian to Bad Dreikirchen's parking on the right (after 1 kilometer). Call the hotel from the village and they will arrange for a taxi.

BAD DREIKIRCHEN
Hosts: Wodenegg family
San Giacomo 6
Barbian, (BZ) 39040, Italy
Tel & fax: (0471) 650055
30 rooms sharing 15 bathrooms
Lire 92,000–148,000 double B&B
 65,000–93,000 per person half board
3-day minimum stay
Breakfast and dinner served
Open May 15 to October 15
English spoken well
Region: Trentino-Alto Adige

The Pomurlo farm, home to the congenial Minghelli family, covers 370 acres of hills, woods, and open fields and is an excellent base for touring Umbria. A winding dirt road leads past the horse stables and riding rings to the typical stone house which contains a restaurant featuring farm-fresh specialties. Inside, the tables are covered with crisp white linen. An antique cupboard and old farm implements on the walls enhance the rustic setting. Three "country suites" are situated beneath the restaurant, each consisting of two bedrooms, bathroom, and kitchenette. Comfortable and cheerful, the suites are decorated with wrought-iron beds, colorful bedspreads, and typical regional country antiques. A nearby converted stall houses two adorable independent rooms looking out over the lake. Other guestrooms and apartments are found in three large hilltop homes commanding a breathtaking view of the entire valley with its grazing herds of longhorn cattle. The main house, a 12th-century tower fortress where the inn's personable hostess Daniela resides, accommodates guests in three additional suites of rooms. Breakfast fixings are provided in rooms. A swimming pool is a welcome addition to the list of activities provided. The farm is conveniently located near the Rome-Florence autostrada. *Directions:* Take the Orvieto exit from the A1 autostrada. Follow signs for Todi, **not** for Baschi. On route N448 turn right at the sign for Pomurlo.

POMURLO VECCHIO
Hosts: Lazzaro Minghelli & family
Localita: Lago di Corbara
Baschi (TR) 05023, Italy
Tel: (0744) 950190/950475 Fax: (0744) 950500
15 rooms and suites, most with private bathrooms
Lire 65,000–80,000 per person half board
Trattoria on premises
Open all year
Some English spoken
Region: Umbria

The Locanda, a pale-yellow-and-brick villa dating from 1830, sits on the border between Tuscany and Umbria and is an excellent base from which to explore this rich countryside. The villa's dining room features a vaulted ceiling in toast-colored brick, an enormous fireplace, French windows opening out to the flower garden, and antiques including a cupboard adorned with the family's blue-and-white china. The upstairs quarters are reserved primarily for guests, and contain five comfortable rooms and an inviting sitting room and library. The cozy bedrooms have mansard ceilings, armoires, lovely linens, and washbasins. A suite and an additional guestroom are located on the ground floor in the opposite wing. These accommodations, each with private bath, are decorated with antique reproductions and appear more modern. The young hostess, Palmira, is a wonderful regional cook and enjoys giving informal lessons free of charge to her guests. She has just opened the dining room to non-guests as well. Siena is only 45 kilometers away, and the quaint medieval and Renaissance villages of Pienza, Montepulciano, and Montalcino are close by. *Directions:* Exit from the Rome-Florence autostrada at Val di Chiana. Head toward Bettolle, then bear right toward Siena. Follow signs for La Bandita.

LOCANDA LA BANDITA
Hostess: Palmira Fiorini
Via Bandita 72
Bettolle-Sinalunga (SI) 53040, Italy
Tel & fax: (0577) 624649
7 rooms with private bathrooms
Lire 120,000 double B&B
* 85,000 per person half board*
Breakfast and dinner served
Open all year
Credit cards: all major
English spoken well
Region: Tuscany

This guide includes some small bed-and-breakfast-like urban hotels for the convenience of travelers who would like to do some metropolitan sightseeing. For some reason, the city of Bologna is often bypassed by visitors, despite its rich past, beautiful historic center, arcaded streets, and elegant shops. Cristina and Mauro Orsi, the owners of the splendid Hotel Corona d'Oro, mentioned in another of our guides, *Italy: Charming Inns & Itineraries,* own two other centrally located, smaller hotels: the Orologio and the Commercianti. Just steps away from Bologna's main piazza and basilica you find the recently renovated Orologio, so-called because it looks onto city hall with its clock tower. The hotel has thirty-one rooms, and one apartment, on three floors, and the intimate atmosphere of a family-run establishment. The newly remodeled guestrooms are pleasantly decorated with pretty floral-print wallpaper, photographs of the city from the 1930s, and simple reproduction furniture. An unusual but welcome treat is the full breakfast buffet served in the dining room. Signor Orsi's other "urban inn," the modern Hotel Commercianti around the corner, is being remodeled with the objective of having the decor more closely reflect the building's 13th-century vintage. The owners also organize personalized cooking classes and private tours of Bologna and surrounding cities.

Directions: Located in the heart of the old city.
HOTEL OROLOGIO
Hostess: Cristina Orsi
Via IV Novembre 10
Bologna 40123, Italy
Tel: (051) 231253 Fax: (051) 260552
31 rooms with private bathrooms, 1 apartment
Lire 250,000–275,000 double B&B
Breakfast only
Credit cards: all major
Open all year
English spoken well
Region: Emilia-Romagna

A pocket of absolutely stunning yet unexplored countryside is the Oltrepo Pavese hills, 60 kilometers south of Milan. It is predominantly wine country producing top-quality Cortese, Pinot, Barbera, and Riesling. Less than an hour's drive away is the Alba/Asti wine region of Piemont and the Italian Riviera. Also not to be missed is historic Pavia and its celebrated Certosa monastery. What better place to set up a home base than the Castello di Stefanago where a variety of accommodation is available. The two Baruffaldi brothers work diligently at producing wines and maintaining their 600-acre property. The 12th-century castle perched atop a hill and taking in spectacular views houses the host families and five lovely apartments for two to five persons. Each has a bathroom, living area, and kitchenette and has been decorated appropriately with the family's period furniture. Below the castle on the road is a restored farmhouse "La Boatta" (don't let the neon sign left by past owners throw you off) where a restaurant and six sweet double bedrooms are available. Each room has coordinated Provençal-patterned spreads and curtain with spotless bathrooms. Typical meals are served using fresh produce directly from the farm. *Directions*: Exit at Bereguardo/Pavia on the A7 autostrada from Milan. Follow it to Pavia (skirting the city)and then Casteggio. Drive on to Montebello-Schizzola-Arpesina and up the long drive to the castle.

CASTELLO DI STEFANAGO **NEW**
Hosts: Giacomo Baruffaldi
Borgo Priolo (PV) 27040, Italy
Tel & fax: (0383) 875227 or 875413
6 rooms with private bathrooms, 5 apartments
Lire 80,000 double B&B
 75,000 per person half board
All meals served
Open March to October
Very good English spoken
Region: Lombardy

Just off the busy road that connects the major towns of Umbria—Perugia, Assisi, Spoleto, and Todi—is the elegant country house Giulia, which has been in the Petrucci family since its 14th-century origins. Later additions were built on to the stone villa, one of which Signora Caterina has opened up to guests. Time seems to have stood still in the six bedrooms, all but one with en-suite bathroom, and filled with grandmother Giulia's lovely antique iron-wrought beds, armoires, and period paintings. They are divided between three floors, accessed by a steep stone staircase, the largest having a ceiling fresco depicting the local landscape. Breakfast is served either in the chandeliered dining room upstairs, with Oriental carpets, lace curtains, and a large fireplace, or under the oak trees in the front garden during the warmer months. Part of the barn has been recently converted into two independent units which include a fully-equipped kitchenette for up to four persons. Although the large swimming pool overlooks a rather barren field and the distant main road, it is a welcome respite after a full day of touring, which guests will be doing a lot of from this strategically convenient location. *Directions:* Just off the Perugia-Spoleto route 75 between Trevi and Campello.

CASA GIULIA
Hostess: Caterina Alessandrini Petrucci
Via SS Flaminia km.140.1
Bovara di Trevi (PG) 06039, Italy
Tel: (0742) 78257 Fax: (0742) 381632
6 rooms, 5 with private bathrooms
2 apartments
Lire 145,000 double B&B
Breakfast only
Open all year
Some English spoken
Region: Umbria

Brisighella is a gem. The town comes to life during June and July with its annual Medieval Festival when games of the period are re-enacted, and medieval music, literature, and dance are produced. Locals attire themselves in appropriate costume and the village's narrow streets are illuminated nightly by torches for the occasion. Just out of town, past the thermal hot springs, sits the sweet home of a young Milanese couple, Ettore and Adriana, with its 10 hectares of vineyards and orchards. Guests are treated to the host's excellent Sangiovese and Chardonnay wines. The Matareses have renovated the barn next to their small stone house, creating three guestrooms as well as a rustic dining area with exposed beams and a large fireplace where guests gather for typical Romagna-style meals. Rooms are decorated with simple country furnishings. The atmosphere is casual and the value excellent. While in the vicinity don't miss the mosaics in Ravenna, the historical center of Bologna, and the international ceramic museum in Faenza. *Directions:* Take the Faenza exit from the A14 between Bologna and Rimini. Follow signs for Brisighella or Firenze. At town take a left turn for Terme/Modigliona. Il Palazzo is the third house on the left after the Hotel Terme.

IL PALAZZO
Hosts: Ettore Matarese family
Via Baccagnano 11
Brisighella (RA) 48013, Italy
Tel: (0546) 80338
3 rooms, 2 with private bathrooms, 1 apartment
Lire 77,000 double B&B
66,000 per person half board
3-day minimum stay or 20% surcharge
All meals served
Open all year
English spoken well
Region: Emilia-Romagna

The quaint village of Calvi is just on the border between the regions of Lazio and Umbria and conveniently located at 15 kilometers from the autostrada and 70 kilometers from Rome. Sandro and his charming wife, Louise from Sweden, divide their time between Rome and the countryside where their farm's activities include production of wine and olive oil and horse breeding. Their family residence in Calvi is an historic palazzo dating back to the 15th century and filled with period furniture, paintings, and frescoed ceilings. From their windows they look onto the bright yellow farmhouse where hospitality is offered within five comfortable apartments. Accommodations on the first and second floors are a combination of one or two bedrooms, living room with fireplace, fully-equipped kitchen, and bathroom. The house has recently been restored with new bathrooms and tiled floors while maintaining original beamed ceilings and a country flavor in furnishings. Fresh fixings for breakfast are left for guests in the apartments. Besides wandering around the many villages of the Sabina area, you can conveniently visit Orvieto, Todi, and Spoleto, under an hour away. *Directions*: Exit from the Rome-Firenze autostrada A1 at Magliano Sabina. After Magliano, follow signs for Calvi. In town ask for Via Roma.

CASALE SAN MARTINO   **NEW**
Hosts: Louise & Sandro Calza Bini
Via Roma 2a
Calvi (TR) 05032, Italy
Tel: (0744) 710644 or (0368) 435100
5 apartments for 2 to 6 persons
Lire 75,000–200,000 daily per apartment
Weekly stay required July & August
2-day minimum stay
No meals served
Open March to December
English spoken well
Region: Umbria

For those who have a passion for horseback riding, or with an urge to learn, La Mandria provides the opportunity to do either while on holiday. Host and horseman Davide Felice Aondio's horse farm has been in existence for over 30 years and has been a model for riding resorts. Situated near the foothills of the Alps and between the cities of Turin and Milan, the vast, flat property borders a 5,000-hectare national park, offering spectacular scenery and endless possibilities for horseback excursions. The complex is made up of horse stables, indoor/outdoor ring, haylofts, guestrooms, dining room, and the private homes of the proprietor and his son, Marco's, family. The whole forms a square with riding rings in the center. As a national equestrian training center, lessons of every nature are offered for all ages. Six very basic bedrooms with bath are reserved for guests, and good local fare is served in the rustic dining room. Golf, swimming, and tennis facilities are available nearby. Two side trips that must not be missed are first, to lovely Lake Maggiore, and then to the intriguing medieval town of Ricetto where the houses and streets are made of smooth stones. *Directions:* Take the Carisio exit from the Milan-Turin autostrada. Head toward Biella, but at the town of Candelo turn right for Mottalciata. Mandria is on the right.

LA MANDRIA
Hosts: Marco Aondio family
Candelo (VC) 13062, Italy
Tel & fax: (015) 2536078
6 rooms with private bathrooms
Lire 150,000 double B&B
 125,000 per person half board
All meals served
Open all year
English spoken well
Region: Piedmont

Poetically named after a classic Italian tale by Cesare Pavese, a native of this area, the *Luna e i Falo* (meaning the moon and the fire) farmhouse was lovingly restored by Turin couple Ester and Franco Carnero. The ritual described in the story is still performed in August every year when local farmers burn old grapevines under the full moon in hopes of a good crop. On that night, the bonfires dotting hills surrounding the farm create quite a spectacle. The Carneros' brick home has arched windows and an arcaded front terrace, with three double or triple rooms and one apartment within the villa which they have made available to visitors. For a country home, the spacious living/dining area is elaborately furnished with Renaissance period pieces. The bedrooms reveal a combination of old and new decor and sweeping views of the countryside, known for its wineries. The emphasis at the Luna e i Falo is on the cuisine: the proprietors previously owned a highly regarded restaurant in Turin, and continue to practice their culinary skills, producing delicacies such as excellent handmade pasta. *Directions:* From Asti follow the signs for Canelli and, before town, take a right up the hill to Castello Gancia. The farmhouse is on the right after Aie.

LA LUNA E I FALO
Hosts: Ester & Franco Carnero
Localita Aie 37, Canelli (AT) 14053, Italy
Tel: (0141) 831643 Fax: (0141) 823209
3 rooms with private bathrooms
1 apartment for 4 persons
Lire 140,000 double B&B
* 110,000 per person half board*
2-day minimum stay
Breakfast and dinner served
Open all year
No English spoken (French)
Region: Piedmont

North of Florence between Prato and Pistoia is a pocket of little-known, yet entrancing countryside comprising the Calvana mountains and Bisenzio valley. Grazia, Mario, and their three children have lived there all their lives and love sharing their enthusiasm for the area by offering accommodation to visitors. Although the entrance and exterior leave a little to be desired in terms of aesthetics, the property is beautifully situated overlooking a wooded valley and private lake at the back. What really counts here is the hosts' warmth and their sincere effort to make their guests feel at home. The bedrooms for two to three persons with accompanying immaculate baths are sweet and simple, decorated with comfortable, old-fashioned furniture. Guests convene downstairs for breakfast and dinner in the rustic dining room with exposed beams and fireplace. Off the dining room is the kitchen, where you can watch Grazia rolling out fresh pasta for meals which reflect the influence of the bordering regions of Tuscany and Emilia. A visit to the welcoming Ponte alla Villa offers an opportunity to familiarize yourself with the customs of an area off the beaten track. *Directions:* From Prato, take route 325 north for 25 kilometers to Vernio, then bear left toward Cantagallo. Watch for signs for the bed and breakfast at Luicciana.

PONTE ALLA VILLA
Hosts: Grazia Gori & Mario Michelagnoli
Localita: Luicciana 273-La Villa
Cantagallo (FI) 50040, Italy
Tel: (0574) 956094/956244
8 rooms with private bathrooms
Lire 70,000 double B&B (2-day minimum stay)
  50,000 per person half board
All meals served
Open all year—weekends only during winter
Very little English spoken
Region: Tuscany

La Minerva is located in a quiet section of Capri, slightly off the beaten track, yet still quite central, permitting easy access to the more bustling areas of town—a walker's paradise with no motorized transportation allowed. The street-level entrance is the hotel's third-floor living room, a vast chamber with stark-white tiled floors and ground-to-ceiling windows overlooking the sea. This captivating view will strike you every time you come and go, or eat breakfast, as the same panorama greets you in the dining room. The rest of the small hotel is beneath, with the reception and breakfast area on the ground floor. Signora Esposito has decorated the 18 rooms sweetly and simply with colorful tiled floors and scattered antiques. Each bedroom has a private balcony overlooking umbrella-pine woods and the sea. All rooms also have their own bath, done in blue and white tile. The family lives in one section of the building, but share with guests their homey living room, with family photos and lace doilies on the tables. This is a peaceful spot to get away, but not too far away. *Directions:* It's best to stop by the tourist office as you get off the ferry and get a map of Capri, showing the Via Occhio Marino.

LA MINERVA
Hosts: Luigi Esposito family
Via Occhio Marino 8
Capri (NA) 80073, Italy
Tel: (081) 8377067 Fax: (081) 8375221
18 rooms with private bathrooms
Lire 170,000–200,000 double B&B
Breakfast only
Open Easter to October
Credit cards: all major
Some English spoken
Region: Campania

The Villa Krupp is a pleasant small hotel whose claim to local fame can be found in its guest book, boasting such illustrious names as Lenin and Gorky. Signor Coppola, the cordial and proud proprietor, took over the property in 1964. The charming hotel contains 12 bedrooms, each with its own bath, in a somewhat modern and boxy building alongside the host's own residence. The Krupp is dramatically situated in one of the most beautiful corners of Capri's Augusto Park, atop a steep, sheer cliff dropping to the sparkling turquoise sea beneath. The site overlooks the Faraglioni rock formation (a symbol of the island) and Marina Piccola, one of Capri's two ports. A thousand steps lead from its top edge down to the seaside. The Villa Krupp has its own set of steps leading up to the best vantage point from which to admire this spectacular panorama. The light-filled guestrooms, each featuring its own terrace and bath, are decorated with simple antiques and tiled with the brightly colored ceramics typical of Capri. Room number 18 is a particular favorite due to its relatively large sea-view terrace. Breakfast is served on the veranda or outside on the flowered terrace. *Directions:* Take the cable car up to Capri, walk through the main square, then down the Via Emanuele to Matteotti (on the right).

VILLA KRUPP
Hosts: Coppola family
Viale Matteotti 12
Capri (NA) 80073, Italy
Tel: (081) 8370362 or 8377473
Fax: (081) 8376489
12 rooms with private bathrooms
Lire 160,000–210,000 double B&B
Breakfast only
Open all year
Some English spoken
Region: Campania

Capri has long had a reputation for being an exclusive island and with prices substantially higher than the rest of the country, only the elite were able to afford to vacation there. However, the cost of tourism across Italy has soared, bringing other destinations more in line with Capri in terms of expense, therefore making it relatively more affordable than it once was. Unfortunately, agritourism does not exist on the island, but there are several small, family-run hotels that provide a bed-and-breakfast "feeling." One such establishment belongs to Antonino Vuotto and his wife, a local couple who have opened up their centrally located, prim white home in the town of Capri, making four bedrooms available to guests. The rooms are very clean and neat, with typically tiled floors, and private baths and balconies in each. Some even have a view of the sea. Breakfast is not served because there are no common rooms for guests. The Villa's convenient location makes it easy to get to any of Capri's fine restaurants for breakfast, lunch and dinner. *Directions:* Take the cable car up to Capri. Go through the main town square to Via Emanuele, past the Quisisana Hotel and continue to the end of the street. Turn left onto Via Certosa, then left again on Cerio. The Villa is on the corner and is not marked with a sign.

VILLA VUOTTO
Hosts: Antonino Vuotto family
Via Campo di Teste 2
Capri (NA) 80073, Italy
Tel: (081) 8370230
4 rooms with private bathrooms
Lire 90,000 double (no breakfast)
No meals served
Open all year
Very little English spoken
Region: Campania

The Ombria farmhouse nestles amidst the foothills just 30 kilometers from both beautifully austere Bergamo and Lecco on Lake Como. Bed-and-breakfast/restaurant activity in this 1613 stone house began in 1991 after meticulous restoration by gracious and reserved hosts, Luciano and Adda, who have given great attention to detail and to preserving the original architectural features. An arched entryway leads into a stone courtyard with gazebo and open grill, where tables are set for summer meals. The Ombria is well-known for its exceptional restaurant where locals enjoy candlelit regional cuisine at long tables in the intimate stone-walled dining room—as long as they make reservations three months in advance! The spacious doubles, which accommodate up to four persons, are decorated with country antiques and wrought-iron beds. Original fireplace, exposed beams, warm wood floors, and stone walls make them very appealing and cozy. Luciano has given extra attention to bathrooms which are beautifully tiled and rather luxurious. Readers give a high rating to this special place. *Directions:* From Milan take the A4 autostrada, exit at Agrate and head north toward Lecco on Route 36 through an industrial area. At route 342 turn right toward Caprino Bergamasco and follow signs for Celana and Ombria

OMBRIA
Hosts: Adda & Luciano Marchesin
Localita: Celana
Caprino Bergamasco
(BG) 24030, Italy
Tel: (035) 781668
3 rooms with private bathrooms
Lire 85,000 per person half board
Breakfast and dinner served
Open all year
Some English spoken
Region: Lombardy

West of Chianti, just behind the medieval hilltop village of Casole d'Elsa, and half an hour from picturesque Siena and San Gimignano, sits a typical Tuscan stone farmhouse. The Zito family, who have run a successful bed and breakfast here for the past nine years and have been hosts to many happy American travelers, have just sold the property and passed the activity on to Patrizia and Daniele, a young Swiss-Italian couple. Originally from Northern Italy, and having lived in Switzerland for most of their lives, the couple have decided to return to Italy with their two children and continue where the Zitos left off. The seven guestrooms on the second floor above their living quarters all have spotless blue-and-white-tiled bathrooms and welcoming flowers, and retain a simple country flavor, enhanced by the worn terra-cotta brick floors, beamed ceilings, antique armoires and bedside tables, and wrought-iron beds. The restored barn offers a lovely two-bedroom house for weekly stays. Breakfast consisting of fresh-baked cakes and breads is served until noon outside on the rose-covered stone patio overlooking the sheep-dotted hillsides. *Directions:* From Florence take the superstrada toward Siena, exiting at Colle Val d'Elsa. Take Route 68 and turn left for Casole d'Elsa. The inn is just outside town beyond the Hotel Pietralta.

PODERE CAPRETTO
Hosts: Patrizia & Daniele Jenni
Casole d'Elsa (SI) 53031, Italy
Tel: (0577) 948550
7 rooms with private bathrooms
1 apartment
Lire 110,000 double B&B
Breakfast only
Open all year
English spoken well
Region: Tuscany

A stay at the Villa Aureli with Count and Contessa di Serego Alighieri (descendants of Dante) can only be memorable. With its back to the town and looking out over the Italian Renaissance garden and surrounding countryside, the imposing brick villa has been standing for the past 300 years. When it was bought by the di Serego family in the 18th century, it was meticulously restored and embellished with plasterwork, decorative painted ceilings, richly painted fabrics on walls, ornately framed paintings and prints, colorful tiles from Naples, and Umbrian antiques. Left intentionally intact by the Count, who disdains overly-restored historical homes, the elegant apartments for guests maintain their original ambiance. They can accommodate from four to six persons and are spacious, having numerous sitting rooms with fireplaces. A small swimming pool set against the villa's stone walls is a refreshing spot for dreaming. The villa serves as an ideal base from which to explore Umbria and parts of Tuscany, as well as special local itineraries prepared by the Count. *Directions*: Exit from the Perugia highway at Madonna Alta and follow route 220 for Citta della Pieve. After 6 kilometers, take the left for Castel del Piano.

VILLA AURELI   **NEW**
Hosts: Leonardo di Serego Alighieri family
Via Cirenei 70
Castel del Piano Umbro (PG) 06071, Italy
Tel & fax: (075) 774141 or tel: (075) 5736707
2 apartments
Lire 1,000,000–1,900,000 weekly
No meals served
Open all year
English spoken well
Region: Umbria

What a pleasant surprise to discover the Solarola, a sunny yellow villa as its name implies, in the flat countryside around Bologna. It is, in a word "perfect." Gracious hosts Antonella and Valentino (a renowned architect), took over the family farm several years ago, transforming one of its two turn-of-the-century villas into a private home and the other into a guesthouse with five double rooms, a restaurant, living room, billiard room, and outdoor gazebo and beautiful swimming pool. Eight new rooms were opened last year in the former barn directly in front. Antonella decorated the guest villa to be romantic and refined, yet warm and inviting. Each room is named after a flower and everything from wallpaper, botanical prints, and fluffy comforters to motifs on lampshades and bed frames, bouquets, and even room fragrance conform to the floral theme. Victoriana abounds in details such as cupboards filled with china, lace curtains and doilies, dried-flower bouquets, old family photos, and Tiffany lamps. In addition, Antonella is known for her refined cuisine, creating inventive combinations with the freshest of ingredients. *Directions:* Exit from autostrada A14 at Castel S. Pietro and turn right towards Medicina for 5 kilometers. Turn right at Via S. Paolo, follow the road to the end then turn right again on Via S. Croce to Solarola.

LOCANDA SOLAROLA
Hosts: Antonella Scardovi & Valentino Parmiani
Via San Croce 5
Castel Guelfo (BO) 40023, Italy
Tel: (0542) 670102/670089 Fax: (0542) 670222
13 doubles with private bathrooms
Lire 240,000 double B&B
All meals served
Open all year
Credit cards: all major
Some English spoken
Region: Emilia-Romagna

The Villa Gaidello farm has been written up on several occasions (in *Bon Appetit*, *Cuisine*, *Eating in Italy*), mostly as a result of its superb cuisine. There is nothing extravagant about hostess Paola Bini's recipes, carefully prepared by local women. Rather, the secret to her success seems to lie in the revival of basic traditional dishes using the freshest possible ingredients. Pasta is made daily (a great treat to watch) and features all the local variations on tagliatelle, pappardelle, and stricchettoni. Reservations for dinner must be made several days in advance. Paola was one of the pioneers in agritourism, transforming her grandmother's nearly 200-year-old farmhouse into a guest house and restaurant 20 years ago. One to five guests are accommodated in each of the three suites, which include kitchen and sitting room. The suites are cozy and rustic with exposed-brick walls, country antiques, and lace curtains. The dining room, set with doilies and ceramic, is situated in the converted hayloft and overlooks the vast garden and a small pond. The Gaidello provides a convenient stopover just off the Bologna-Milan autostrada. *Directions:* Exit the autostrada at Castelfranco, Modena Sud. Follow Via Emilia/Route 9, turning left at the sign for Gaidello.

VILLA GAIDELLO
Hostess: Paola Bini
Via Gaidello 18
Castelfranco Emilia (MO) 41013, Italy
Tel: (059) 926806 Fax: (059) 926620
3 suites with private bathrooms
Lire 160,000 double B&B
All meals served
Closed August, restaurant closed Sundays
Credit cards: all major
Very little English spoken
Region: Emilia-Romagna

A really unique stay involving an exceptional culinary experience can be found at the Borgo Villa a Sesta, a complete medieval stone village in the middle of the beautiful countryside of Chianti. The estate produces Chianti wines and olive oil, and offers seven lovely apartments of various sizes within the village. They are all well furnished with a mix of antiques and contain one or two bedrooms, new bathroom, living room, and fully equipped kitchen. Four are situated in a three-story brick house overlooking the vineyards and swimming pool. What really makes the stay here so special is a meal at the nearby Bottega del'30, an intimate eight-table restaurant, well known for its superior cuisine—the two establishments work hand in hand. A meal at Bottega del'30, run by energetic and congenial hosts, Franco Camelia and French-born Helene Stoquelet, is sure to be a memorable event. They have spent the past year developing their newly opened Tuscan cooking school, with both an authentic country kitchen and a fully equipped modern kitchen, which is truly impressive. A lovely dining room with long wood table is where everyone joins together for lunch after a lesson (available weekly or daily). Not to be missed! *Directions*: From Siena on route 73 exit at Castelnuovo Berardenga. Pass the town and continue for San Gusme. Villa a Sesta is on the left 2 kilometers after the turnoff for San Gusme.

BORGO VILLA A SESTA   **NEW**
Host: Oskar Sigrist
Localita: Villa a Sesta
Castelnuovo Berardenga (SI) 53019, Italy
Tel: (0577) 734064
7 apartments for 2 to 6 persons
Lire 180,000–320,000 per apartment
3-day minimum stay, 1 week July & August
Lunch with cooking school, dinner at Bottega del'30
Open all year
Some English spoken
USA Rep: Diana Place (407) 361-0301
Region: Tuscany

The Podere San Quirico is a sweet little Tuscan farmhouse with an even sweeter owner and hostess, Maria Consiglio Picone, a former theater-costume designer who moved to Tuscany from her native Naples 22 years ago. Her bed-and-breakfast activity commenced soon afterward, once the 14th-century crumbling stone farmhouse had been lovingly pieced back together. Maria proudly points out how the original exposed-beam structure dating from 1300 has been kept intact, and how her enchanting informal garden has developed over the years. Six guestrooms in her home are decorated in harmony with the house, containing very simple country furniture and wrought-iron beds. Most rooms have their own bath, as well as a gorgeous view over the soft green countryside. The former horse stalls have been converted into a dining room and kitchen for the convenience of visitors. A separate two-bedroom house is available for weekly stays. Four additional bedrooms with baths should be ready by spring, 1996. Just 14 kilometers from Siena (a must-see destination), and at the foot of the Chianti region, the San Quirico serves as an ideal touring base. *Directions:* Depending on the direction of your approach, exit either at Monte San Savino or Valdarno off the A1 Firenze-Roma highway. Follow signs for Castelnuovo Berardenga. The bed and breakfast is just outside town and well marked.

PODERE SAN QUIRICO
Hostess: Maria Consiglio Picone
Via del Paradiso 1
Castelnuovo Berardenga (SI) 53019, Italy
Tel & fax: (0577) 355206
6 rooms, 4 with private bathrooms
1 apartment
Lire 109,000 double B&B
Breakfast served upon request
Open all year
Some English spoken
Region: Tuscany

To the west of Cortina, the most fashionable ski area in the Dolomites, is Val Gardena, which is almost too storybook-perfect to be true. The valley, once part of Austria, still preserves its Germanic heritage in its language, cuisine, and culture. This adorable bed and breakfast is owned and run by a young local couple with four children. The crisp white house with its old stone-and-wood attached barn has been in the same family for over 400 years and was recently renovated, giving the property a fresh new look. The entrance foyer walls are adorned with antique farm tools, harnesses, and cow bells. On the same floor is a dining room with individual tables where guests enjoy breakfast with a view of the velvet green hillside. The five guestrooms, all but one with private bath, are simply and comfortably furnished with pinewood beds and armoires, bright-orange curtains, and fluffy comforters. Stepping out on the balcony reveals a breathtaking panorama of the pine-covered mountains. The Riers are happy to suggest scenic places to explore by car or on foot, and know the best places for rock climbing up into one of the most spectacular ranges in Europe. *Directions:* Exit at Bolzano Nord from the Verona-Brennero autostrada and follow signs for Siusi. Beyond town, before Castelrotto, turn right for Alps, then left for Marmsolerhof.

MARMSOLERHOF
Hosts: August Rier family
San Valentino 35
Castelrotto (BZ) 39040, Italy
Tel: (0471) 706514
5 rooms, 4 with private bathrooms
Lire 55,000 double B&B
Breakfast only
Open all year
Very little English spoken (German)
Region: Trentino-Alto Adige

Tucked away off a winding mountain road in the enchanting Siusi Alps is a typical Tyrolean farmhouse, called *mas* in this northern region of Alto Adige. The Jaider family has resided here ever since the 15th century, traditionally maintaining a dairy farm. Their inviting home is colorfully accented with green shutters and flower-laden boxes at every window. Two wooden barns are connected to the residence via a stone terrace. Signora Jaider runs her home with the hotel efficiency which has come to be expected by visitors to this predominantly German-speaking area, once belonging to Austria. Meals are served out on the terrace in clement weather, or in the original dining room, whose charm is enhanced by the low, wood-paneled ceiling (so constructed to retain heat) with its hand-painted edelweiss flowers. Cuisine in this region reflects its Austrian heritage, with *speck* ham, meat and potatoes, and apple strudel winning over pasta dishes. Lovely country antiques are dispersed throughout the house and the eight bedrooms, which are wood-paneled from floor to ceiling and have pretty valley views. Two guestrooms include balconies. *Directions:* Exit at Bolzano Nord from autostrada A22, following signs for Fie and Alpe di Siusi. Pass through Siusi and turn off to the left for Tisana. San Osvaldo is on the left after Tisana.

TSCHOTSCHERHOF
Hosts: Jaider family
San Osvaldo 19
Castelrotto (BZ) 39040, Italy
Tel: (0471) 706013
8 rooms with private bathrooms
Lire 65,000 double B&B
* 46,000 per person half board*
All meals served
Open March to October
Very little English spoken (German)
Region: Trebtino-Alto Adige

Liguria is the sliver of a region touching France and boasting the Italian Riviera with its port towns of Portofino, Santa Margherita, San Remo, and Cinque Terre. From the busy coastal town of Sestri Levante, an 8-kilometer rough and winding road leads up a mountain to the rather remote but serene Monte Pu farm, where Aurora and Pino migrated from Milan. The three-story, peach-color brick farmhouse complex, dating from 1400, commands a marvelous sweeping view over wooded mountains and valleys down to the sea. The guestrooms, a combination of triples and quads, are simple and immaculate, with light-pine furniture and wildflower bouquets. Downstairs is the warm and airy dining room where a full country breakfast awaits guests each morning. Dinner, prepared by a local woman, is served outside in the courtyard in warmer months. The culinary emphasis is on vegetarian dishes such as risotto, soups, and salads, prepared with ingredients straight from the garden. Horses are available for riding in the forest preserves surrounding the property. Aurora and Pino take time from their busy schedule of running the farm and looking after a new baby to assist guests with itineraries. *Directions:* Exit from the Genova-Livorno autostrada at Sestri Levante and follow signs for Casarza Ligure. After town turn right for Campegli Massaco and then onward to Monte Pu.

MONTE PU
Hostess: Aurora Giani
Castiglione Chiavarese (GE) 16030, Italy
Tel & fax: (0185) 408027
9 rooms, 5 with private bathrooms
1 apartment
Lire 132,000 double B&B
  110,000 per person half board
All meals served
Open Easter to December
English spoken well
Region: Liguria

On a hilltop in Pomino wine country sits the 15th-century Medici villa belonging to the Nicolodi family, only its third proprietors. Surrounded by hundreds of acres of scenic vineyards, olive groves, and cypress woods, the large ivy-covered villa also features a Renaissance garden with stone statuary. Within the historic villa are six comfortable guestrooms, only one with private bath. Six independent apartments are found in the farmhouses which dot the vast property. With its elaborate, worn antiques, gilt mirrors, period paintings, Oriental carpets, chandeliers, and enormous gray-stone fireplaces, the place seems frozen in time. Yet there is a casual and welcoming atmosphere: the Nicolodis put on no false airs and guests may wander about freely. Signora, who is Neopolitan, as her cooking confirms, and Signor, who has traveled widely, sincerely enjoy receiving guests at home. They have recently organized week-long itineraries including cooking lessons for eight to ten people. With facilities for tennis, swimming, and billiards, a Jacuzzi, beautiful scenery, and excellent meals (including full American-style breakfast), they do a good job of persuading their guests to stay. *Directions:* From Florence follow signs for Pontassieve. After Rufina, turn right for Pomina.

LA SOSTA AI BUSINI
Hosts: Marcello Nicolodi family
Localita Castiglioni di Rufina
Rufina (FI) 50068, Italy
Tel: (055) 8397809 Fax: (055) 8397004
6 rooms, 1 with private bathroom, 6 apartments
Lire 160,000 double B&B (2-day minimum stay)
  110,000 per person half board
All meals served
Open all year
Credit cards: MC, VS
English spoken well
Region: Tuscany

We were delighted to hear that one of our favorite bed-and-breakfast hostesses, the delightful Stella Casolaro, has started another bed and breakfast in her new home after having sold the Scuderia in Badia di Passignano. If you were ever one of her fortunate guests, you would understand why travelers come back and stay with her year after year. Her new location, 35 kilometers west of Siena, is in the lesser-known, more rugged part of the Tuscan countryside. In fact, much to the delight of husband, Carlo, who has a passion for hunting for porcini mushrooms, dense woods cover the entire area. Not to be missed are the mystic ruins of San Galgamo cathedral. The white 60-year-old house with encircling garden is right on the edge of the quaint village of Ciciano. Three sweet bedrooms, each with its own bathroom, and a living room have been reserved for guests on the couple's second floor, while they reside on the third floor. All rooms have a double wrought-iron bed with a variety of country antiques in keeping with the simple yet homey ambiance. At just 2 kilometers from the home is Stella's miniature restaurant, Il Minestraio, where she shows off her talent for pasta and soup dishes. It's like "coming home." *Directions*: From Siena, take route 73 towards Grosseto. After Frosini, turn off to the right for Chiusdino, then Ciciano. Ciciano is 45 kilometers from the seaside.

CASA ITALIA
Hosts: Stella & Carlo Casolaro
Via Massetana 5
Ciciano-Chiusdino (SI) 53010, Italy
Tel: (0577) 750656
3 rooms with private bathrooms
Lire 60,000 double (no breakfast)
Lunch and dinner served in restaurant
Open all year
No English spoken
Region: Tuscany

In 1987 Rosemarie and Filippo bought and restored the elegant 16th-century Villa Montesolare (sun-colored as its name implies), opening its doors just recently to guests. Crowning a summit in unspoiled countryside (on one side—the approach side has unfortunately been invaded with new construction, invisible from the villa) between Umbria and Tuscany, just south of lovely Lake Trasimeno, the villa overlooks its surrounding estate of olive trees and vineyards. A wide gray-stone staircase leads up to the eight guestrooms and two suites, all with private bath and furnished in appropriate period style with carefully selected antiques. Five more suites are located in a 17th-century house on the property. Across from the cozy bar at the entrance, where guests enjoy a cocktail before dinner, is the intimate and elegant frescoed dining room, where fine Tuscan cuisine is presented under Rosemarie's supervision. Guests are made to feel at home, whether relaxing in the impressive powder-blue upstairs salon with glass chandelier and massive stone fireplace, or wandering through the Italian Renaissance lemon-tree garden. Less passive activities include tennis, horseback riding, or swimming in one of the gorgeous hillside pools. *Directions:* From Perugia take N220 toward Citta di Pieve. After Fontignano (3 kilometers), turn right at San Paolo to the villa (4 kilometers).

VILLA DI MONTESOLARE
Hosts: Rosemarie & Filippo Strunk Iannarone
Localita: Colle San Paolo
Panicale (PG) 06064, Italy
Tel: (075) 832376 Fax: (075) 8355462
8 rooms and 7 suites with private bathrooms
Lire 130,000–150,000 per person half board
Breakfast and dinner served
Open all year
Credit cards: MC, VS
English spoken very well
Region: Umbria

Even though the Falconiere is more of a small hotel than a family-run bed and breakfast, it is too irresistible a choice for those who want a first-rate splurge. Romance prevails in this jewel of a place, superbly restored by stunning couple, Silvia and Riccardo, who inherited the property from his grandmother. What was once the stone lemon house is now an elegant vaulted dining room looking out to the stone courtyard accented with colorful roses. Upstairs is the intimate breakfast room with stenciled borders and beamed ceilings. Just a few steps away, hidden among chestnut and olive trees, is the pale-yellow villa where the nine individual guestrooms, each decorated with discerning taste and attention to detail, are situated on three floors. With guests' comfort in mind, 17th-century architecture is discreetly combined with 20th-century amenities. A small but utterly romantic "nest" is tucked within the cupola and offers splendid views of the countryside. From 1848 to 1858 this was the residence of Italian poet, Antonio Guadagnoli. If all of this isn't enough to tempt you, either Silvia's exquisite cuisine or Riccardo's poetry reading will certainly do it. Enchanting. *Directions*: From the A1 autostrada (Firenze-Roma), exit at Valdichiana and follow the road for Cortona. Instead of going up to town, follow route 71 for Arezzo where you see signs for Il Falconiere.

IL FALCONIERE   **NEW**
Hosts: Silvia & Riccardo Baracchi
Localita San Martino 43
Cortona (AR) 52044, Italy
Tel: (0575) 612679 Fax: (0575) 612927
9 rooms with private bathrooms, 3 suites
Lire 250,000 double B&B
All meals served
Open all year
Credit cards: all major
English spoken well
Region: Tuscany

For British couple, Scarlett and Colin, the fantasy of restoring a farmhouse in the hills of Tuscany and blending into the slower-paced life of local farmers became reality seven years ago when they found the property of their dreams. Remotely set amongst the lush green mountains separating Tuscany and Umbria, the ancient stone farmhouse was meticulously restored and tastefully appointed with country antiques and matching fabrics. Within are the hosts' quarters plus two lovely guestrooms on the first floor. Scarlett, an excellent cook, prepares light lunches or occasional dinners accompanied by top-choice local wines. Two kilometers away is a four-bedroom residence that the couple rents out weekly. This is an ideal place for those who like to combine leisurely local touring with pure relaxation, taking advantage of the lovely swimming pool with the most incredible views over the valley. *Directions*: Exit from the A1 autostrada at Val di Chiana and follow the highway towards Perugia. Exit at the second turnoff for Cortona, pass the city, and continue for Citta del Castello on a small winding (very scenic) road. After 5 kilometers turn left at Portole and call the hotel for instructions on how to find the unmarked dirt road to the house. Thirty minutes from Cortona.

STOPPIACCE **NEW**
Hosts: Scarlett & Colin Campbell
Localita: San Pietro a Dame
Cortona (AR) 52044, Italy
Tel & fax: (0575) 690058
2 bedrooms with private bathrooms
1 house (4 bedrooms)
Lire 160,000 double B&B
* 1,200,000–2,200,000 weekly (house)*
2-day minimum stay
Breakfast and occasional dinner served
Open March to October
Fluent English spoken
Region: Tuscany

English bed-and-breakfast owner, Sarah Townsend, a true Italiophile, and her husband Johnny have poured their heart and soul into making Il Bacchino a veritable cultural, epicurean, and visual feast. A mere ten-minute walk from the fine antique center of Cortona, this small but beautiful 17th-century villa has been lovingly restored to its former glory. The original interior with its wood beams, vaulted ceilings, and stone floors is filled with elegant period antiques and paintings. Sarah's open-house philosophy allows guests to lounge in any of the three cozy sitting rooms or outside on the wicker sofas overlooking her marvelous terraced 17th-century Italian garden—just another one of her many talents. A spectacular mosaic swimming pool is perched on the upper terrace surrounded by breathtaking countryside views. Four sweetly decorated guest bedrooms are on the second floor along with an inviting living room displaying trompe l'oeil designs by Sarah. A lovely sideboard filled with a collection of blue-and-white china dominates the dining room where guests are treated to innovative meals prepared by daughter, Honor, who has a wealth of international culinary skills. Their former farmhouse ten minutes away is available for weekly rentals. *Directions*: Since there are no signs, it is best to call when you reach the center of Cortona.

VILLA IL BACCHINO
Hosts: Sarah & Johnny Townsend
Torreone 126
Cortona (AR) 52044, Italy
Tel & fax: (0575) 603284
4 rooms, 3 with private bathrooms
Lire 220,000 double B&B
3-day minimum stay
Breakfast and dinner served
Open April to November
Fluent English spoken
Region: Tuscany

The Antica Fattoria came highly recommended by several readers who stayed there in the past year since it opened. It is indeed a delightful combination of pretty countryside, strategic touring position, comfortable rooms, excellent meals, and warm hospitality. Following the increasingly popular lifestyle trend of abandoning the city for a rural pace, Roman couple Alessandro and Anna left their offices to become, essentially, farmers. They bought and restored two connected stone farmhouses and incorporated seven rooms, decorated pleasantly with a characteristic country flavor, for guests. While Alessandro tends to the crops, Anna lives out her passion for cooking, much to guests' delight. Meals are served either outside at one long table or in the transformed horse stalls below with cozy sitting area and fireplace. At times the *allegria* and good food keep guests at the table until the wee hours. A lovely swimming pool looks over the wooded hills to the valley. The hosts take time out of their busy schedule to assist guests with the many local itineraries and organize a wide variety of games. Perfect for families and a great base from which to explore Umbria. The town of Deruta is world-famous for its painted ceramic pottery and is lined with shop after shop. *Directions*: From Perugia (18 kilometers), exit from route 3bis at Casalina. Take the first right and follow signs to the Fattoria.

ANTICA FATTORIA DEL COLLE   **NEW**
Hosts: Anna & Alessandro Coluccelli
Strada Colle delle Forche 6
Deruta (PG) 06053, Italy
Tel & fax: (075) 972201
7 rooms with private bathrooms
Lire 90,000 double B&B
  85,000 per person half board
All meals served
Open all year
English spoken well
Region: Umbria

Picturesque Courmayeur, on the Italian side of the tunnel cutting through Mont Blanc into France, is a popular ski and summer resort. In the summer months comfortable temperatures and spectacular mountain scenery along with activities such as hiking, golf, horseback riding, and kayaking attract many visitors. The warm Berthod family have been offering hospitality to guests for some time, greeting them by name as they return "home" year after year. The old stone chalet and barn, squeezed between other houses in the center of the centuries-old village, Entreves, outside Courmayeur, has been recently restored using old and new materials. The cozy reception area maintains its original rustic flavor with flagstone floors and beams, hanging brass pots, typical locally-made pine furniture, and homey touches like dried flower arrangements and lace curtains. The 23 simply appointed rooms have been divided between two buildings and offer amenities of a standard hotel. A hearty breakfast is the only meal served; however, half-board arrangements can be made with local restaurants for longer stays. La Grange is an efficiently-run bed and breakfast right at the foot of the snow-capped Alps. *Directions*: From Aosta where autostrada A5 ends, continue on route 26 to Courmayeur. Entreves is 5 kilometers beyond.

LA GRANGE
Hosts: Berthod family
Fraz. Entreves
Courmayeur (AO) 11013, Italy
Tel: (0165) 869733 Fax: (0165) 869744
23 rooms with private bathrooms
Lire 155,000 double B&B (high season)
Breakfast only
Closed: May, June, October, November
Credit Cards: AX, VS
English spoken well
Region: Valle d'Aosta

Simona and Luciano Nenna relocated to this idyllic spot, surrounding themselves with hundreds of acres of woods, rivers, valleys, and, best of all, utter tranquillity. This ambitious and hospitable couple have restored an isolated village of 12 stone houses, transforming it into a rustic retreat. Besides producing all their own fruits and vegetables, their main activity is equestrian, with 20 horses, well-equipped stables, indoor and outdoor rings, a riding school, and organized excursions into the scenic countryside. The Noci house contains seven simple rooms with private bathrooms, which retain their original terra-cotta floors and wood-beamed ceilings, and are decorated with country furniture. La Terrazza, originally a hunting lodge, houses nine guestrooms with bath, including its namesake terrace room. Other buildings are La Quercia, the dining hall where guests share hearty Umbrian specialties at long tables, and the bar with huge fireplace and occasional live entertainment. Other activities include on-site tennis and swimming. *Directions*: Exit at Fabro from the Rome-Firenze A1 autostrada. Follow signs for Parrano, (7 kilometers), turning right at the Casella sign, and continue for another 7 kilometers on a rough gravel road.

LA CASELLA
Hosts: Simona & Luciano Nenna
Ficulle (TR) 05016, Italy
Tel: (0763) 86075 Fax: (0763) 86684
28 rooms with private bathrooms
Lire 130,000–140,000 per person half board
1 week minimum stay July and August
All meals served
Closed January
Credit cards: all major
Fluent English spoken
Region: Umbria

The Hotel Aprile, owned by the Cantini Zucconi family for the past 35 years, is located in a 15th-century Medici palace behind the Piazza Santa Maria Novella, near the train station and many fine restaurants and shops. The historical building was restored under the strict ordinance of Florence's Commission of Fine Arts. The small and charming hotel is full of delightful surprises: from 16th-century paintings and a bust of the Duke of Tuscany to the frescoed breakfast room and quiet courtyard garden. The old-fashioned reception and sitting areas are invitingly furnished with Florentine Renaissance antiques, comfy, overstuffed red armchairs, and Oriental carpets worn with time. The wallpapered bedrooms include telephone and mini-bar, and feature parquet floors and high vaulted ceilings, but vary widely in their size and decor; some are too basic and modern. There are twenty-four doubles with private bathrooms, and another five which share two bathrooms just outside the rooms. Request one of the quieter rooms at the back of the hotel, overlooking the garden. *Directions:* Use a detailed city map to locate the hotel, three blocks north of the Duomo. There is a parking garage.

HOTEL APRILE
Hosts: Valeria Cantini Zucconi family
Via della Scala 6
Florence 50123, Italy
Tel: (055) 216237 Fax: (055) 280947
29 rooms, 24 with private bathrooms
Lire 215,000 double B&B
Breakfast only
Open all year
Credit cards: all major
English spoken well
Region: Tuscany

The relaxed and friendly Ariele Hotel has been in the Bertelloni family for the past 40 years. Located in a quiet residential section across from the Opera House, it is within a short walking distance to the center of town. The entrance and reception area is made up of several old-fashioned-style sitting rooms, giving an immediate sense of the private home it used to be (dating back to 14th century). These spaces include a breakfast room and wallpapered sitting room with antique reproductions, gold velvet armchairs, fireplace, and Oriental carpets on tiled floors. A pleasant side garden with white iron-wrought tables and chairs offers a shady spot for breakfast. There is also space here for parking at a minimal charge and hidden off in a corner is an unusual independent double room. The spacious, high-ceilinged rooms are individually decorated using a mix of old and new furnishings and have either wood parquet or marble floors. Unfortunately the fluorescent lighting does not help brighten up the sometimes drab color scheme. Guests can depend on the kind assistance of the staff for restaurant and itinerary suggestions. *Directions:* Between Piazza Vittorio Veneto and the Arno river. Use a detailed city map to locate the hotel.

HOTEL ARIELE
Hosts: Bertelloni family
Via Magenta 11
Florence 50123, Italy
Tel: (055) 211509 Fax: (055) 26852
40 rooms with private bathrooms
Lire 195,000 double B&B
Breakfast only
Open all year
Credit cards: VS
English spoken well
Region: Tuscany

If you are facing the Florence train station, a block to the right is the Via Fiume. At the end of this tranquil street you find the Hotel Desiree, located on the upper floors of a building (as is typical of city pensione) and owned and operated by gracious Graziella Pili. Eighteen double rooms are contained within, off a long, gleaming marble hallway wide enough to include a desk and two overstuffed armchairs. Each room has a new bathroom, high ceiling, patterned, polished tile floor, TV, and telephone. The guestrooms are simply decorated with painted furniture and the occasional antique. From the small entrance area, stained glass doors lead to the sweet breakfast room with its pink linen tablecloths topped with fresh bouquets, and out onto its flower-laden balcony overlooking the famous terra-cotta rooftops of Florence—among them that belonging to the glorious Duomo. Signora Pili takes visible pride in her newly renovated hotel and keeps it in immaculate condition. The two-star Hotel Desiree maintains high standards and an economical rate, a combination not easy to find. *Directions:* Use a detailed city map to locate. Parking facilities are available.

HOTEL DESIREE
Hosts: Graziella Pili & Ferdinando Cellini
Via Fiume 20
Florence 50123, Italy
Tel: (055) 2382382 Fax: (055) 291439
18 rooms with private bathrooms
Lire 135,000 double B&B
Breakfast only
Open all year
Credit cards: MC, VS
Some English spoken
Region: Tuscany

The Hotel Hermitage is a dream of a small, well-manicured hotel with efficient service and breathtaking views over the city's most famous monuments. The location could not be more central—on a small street between the Uffizzi gallery and the River Arno. Housed in a 13th-century palazzo, the fifth-floor reception area looking out to the Ponte Vecchio bridge has a cozy living-room feeling with selected antique pieces, Oriental rugs, and corner fireplace. Across the hall is the veranda-like breakfast room dotted with crisp yellow tablecloths and topped with fresh flowers where privileged guests view the tower of Palazzo Signoria. Color-coordinated, separate air-conditioned rooms, recently renovated, have scattered antiques, framed etchings of the city, and more views. However, the highlight of a stay at the Hermitage is spending time dreaming on the rooftop terrace. The view embraces not only the previously mentioned marvels of Florence, but also the famous dome of the Duomo cathedral and Giotto's tower. Guests are served a Continental breakfast under the ivy-covered pergola and among the many flower-laden vases lining its borders. Reserve well in advance. *Directions:* Consult a detailed city map. There is a parking garage in the vicinity. Call for instructions as car traffic in this part of the city is strictly limited.

HOTEL HERMITAGE
Director: Vincenzo Scarcelli
Piazza del Pesce
Florence 50122, Italy
Tel: (055) 287216 Fax: (055) 212208
29 rooms with private bathrooms
Lire 260,000 double B&B
Breakfast only
Open all year
Credit cards: MC, VS
English spoken well
Region: Tuscany

It is not hard to find accommodations in a 15th-century palace in downtown Florence; the historical center of the city has little else. The Residenza is no exception, but it features the added attraction of being situated on Florence's most elegant street, the Tornabuoni. For the last fifteen years the gracious Giacalone family has occupied the palazzo's top three floors and operated them as a pensione (now a hotel). An antique elevator takes you up to the reception area, which opens onto a pretty dining room with pink tablecloths and shelves lined with a collection of bottles, vases, and ceramics. Twenty-four comfortably worn, very simply furnished rooms are divided between the next two floors (the upper floor being the most desirable), capped with a rooftop terrace burgeoning with flowerpots and surrounded by city views. Room decor differs quite a bit as they are in the gradual process of being upgraded with good antique reproductions and air conditioning. A comfortable sitting room with high, beamed ceilings and a television for guests is located on the upper floor. La Residenza is one of the few small hotels offering dinner on the premises, and it is well-known for its authentic Florentine cuisine. *Directions:* Use a detailed city map to locate the hotel in the heart of Florence.

LA RESIDENZA
Hosts: Gianna & Paolo (son) Giacalone
Via Tornabuoni 8
Florence 50123, Italy
Tel: (055) 218684 Fax: (055) 284197
24 rooms with private bathrooms
Lire 215,000 double B&B
  142,500 per person half board
Breakfast and dinner served
Open all year
Credit cards: all major
English spoken well
Region: Tuscany

The newly refurbished Hotel Silla is located on the left bank of the River Arno opposite Santa Croce, the famous 13th-century square and church where Michelangelo and Galileo are buried. This position offers views from some of the rooms of several of Florence's most notable architectural attractions—the Duomo, the Ponte Vecchio, and the tower of Palazzo Vecchio. Housed on the second and third floors of a lovely 15th-century palazzo with courtyard entrance, 39 very new and spotless double rooms with private baths are pleasantly decorated with simple dark-wood furniture and matching bedspreads and curtains. Air conditioning was a recently added necessity. The fancy, cream-colored reception area is appointed in 17th-century Venetian style, with period furniture, chandelier and large paintings. Breakfast is served on the splendid and spacious second-floor outdoor terrace or in the dining room overlooking the Arno. The Silla is a friendly, convenient, and quiet hotel, near the Pitti Palace, leather artisan shops, and many restaurants. It offers tourists a good value in pricey Florence. Garage service is available. *Directions:* Refer to a detailed city map to locate the hotel.

HOTEL SILLA
Host: Gabriele Belotti
Via dei Renai 5
Florence 50125, Italy
Tel: (055) 2342888 Fax: (055) 2341437
39 rooms, 30 with private bathrooms
Lire 200,000 double B&B
Breakfast only
Open all year
Credit cards: all major
English spoken well
Region: Tuscany

The Hotel Splendor is exactly as its name implies—splendid. Off on a quiet side street, the Splendor manages to miss most of the city center's traffic and street noise, yet guests are still able to walk almost everywhere, since the hotel is only three blocks from the Duomo and near the Accademia museum with its *David.* The prim, centuries-old palazzo, of the pale-yellow hue characteristic of Florence, has geranium-filled boxes at every window. The ambiance is reminiscent of a time-worn elegant private home, with its frescoed foyer and sitting rooms graced with portraits, chandeliers, overstuffed armchairs, and Oriental carpets. In summer, the perfume of the family's own garden roses—found throughout the hotel—fills the air. On the second and third floors are the 31 spacious guestrooms (a few can sleep a family of four), some with air conditioning. Most were recently redecorated with lovely matching armoires and beds in typical Florentine painted, pastel style. Perhaps the architectural highlight is the gracious breakfast room, with high ceilings, parquet floors, and frescoed panels all around. French doors lead from this area to an outdoor terrace with white iron chairs and tables where guests may take in a lovely view of San Marco church while enjoying a superb buffet breakfast. Garage service is also available. *Directions:* Rely on a detailed city map to locate the hotel.

HOTEL SPLENDOR
Hosts: Vincenzo Masoero family
Via San Gallo 30
Florence 50129, Italy
Tel: (055) 483427 Fax: (055) 461276
31 rooms, 25 with private bathrooms
Lire 180,000 double B&B, 120,000 without bath
Breakfast only
Open all year
Credit cards: all major
English spoken well
Region: Tuscany

On the border of Umbria and the Marches regions, within reach of the unforgettably romantic towns of Spoleto, Todi, Assisi, and Perugia, is Francesco Rambotti's 18th-century stone farmhouse, beautifully situated atop a hill overlooking the peaceful countryside. Aside from wine-producing grapes, the farm raises deer, sheep, and mountain goats, which roam freely on the property. The University of Perugia conducts research here as a model of farm activity perfectly in tune with the conservation of the environment. The tavern-like dining room has a fireplace, exposed-beamed ceiling, long wood tables, and walls lined with wine casks. Hearty regional fare is served here, complemented by the farm's own wine. Guest accommodation is provided in the house with six double rooms all with private bath, or alternately, two, two-bedroom apartments with bath and kitchenette. The furnishings are spartan and utilitarian, some with bunkbeds for families, and the baths are new and immaculate. They are now producing natural creams and cosmetics at the farm using soil which is said to have been used in ancient times. This part of the country is loaded with must-see destinations, and La Valle offers an inexpensive base from which to explore them. *Directions:* From the Spoleto-Foligno road, turn right at La Valle 7 kilometers after the town of Nocera.

VILLA DELLA CUPA
Host: Francesco Rambotti
Via Colle di Nocera Umbra 141
Gaifana (PG) 06020, Italy
Tel: (0742) 810329 Fax: (0742) 810666
6 rooms with private bathrooms, 2 apartments
Lire 70,000 double B&B
* 55,000 per person half board*
All meals served
Open all year
Credit cards: AX
Very little English spoken
Region: Umbria

The Castello di Tornano, a strategically situated hilltop tower dating back almost 1,000 years, has a 360-degree vista of the surrounding valley and has been of great historical significance in the seemingly endless territorial battles between the Siena and Florence. The current owners are the Selvolini family from Florence, whose lovely daughters, Patrizia and Barbara, opened the wine estate to guests five years ago. Weekly stays begin with meeting other guests around the exquisite pool cut into the rock and spanned by a bridge. Eight simply appointed apartments, each with living area, kitchen, one or two bedrooms, and garden, are situated in a stone farmhouse in front of the tower. The living room in the villa is one of the common areas where guests can gather together. The *pièce de résistance*, however, is the three-floor apartment within the monumental tower, impeccably furnished in grand style and featuring three bedrooms, two living rooms with fireplace, dining room, kitchen, and tower-top terrace with a view not easily forgotten. Meals can be taken at the restaurant on the property. *Directions:* From Siena follow signs for Gaiole (25 kilometers). Continue past town for 5 kilometers, then just past the Lecchi turnoff (on the left), turn right for Tornano-Guarnelotto Ristorante.

CASTELLO DI TORNANO
Hosts: Patrizia & Barbara Selvolini
Localita: Lecchi
Gaiole in Chianti (SI) 53013, Italy
Tel: (0577) 746067 or (055) 6580918
Fax: (0577) 746094
9 apartments
Lire 600,000–2,900,000 (tower) weekly
Trattoria on premises
Open Easter to October and Christmas
Credit cards: AX
English spoken very well
Region: Tuscany

The heel of Italy offers a wealth of natural beauty, but, because its remoteness, few really charming places to stay. The Masseria Lo Prieno is run by the delightful Castriota family, whose crops are representative of the staples of the Apulia region, and include olives, almonds, fruits, and grains. Spartan accommodations are offered in bungalows scattered among the pine woods and palms on the family property. Each guesthouse includes two bedrooms, kitchen, bathroom, and an eating area containing basic necessities. What were formerly animal stalls have been converted into a large dining space rustically decorated with antique farm tools and brass pots. Along with warm hospitality, the family makes the kitchen's offerings a top priority. For an exquisite and authentic traditional meal, the restaurant here is incomparable. Both Maria Grazia, the energetic daughter who runs the show, and her charming mother take pride in demonstrating how local specialties are prepared. This is a budget choice for touring this area. *Directions:* From Taranto take N174 to Galatone, then follow signs for Secli. Turn right on Via Gramsci, then left on Via San Luca. Follow signs for Lo Prieno. 80 kilometers from Brindisi.

MASSERIA LO PRIENO
Hosts: Francesco Castriota family
Localita: Contrada Orelle
Galatone (LE) 73044, Italy
Tel: (0833) 861391/865443
Fax: (0833) 282859
9 bungalows
Lire 60,000 double B&B
* 50,000 per person half board*
Breakfast and dinner served
Open April to September
Some English spoken
Region: Apulia

For the fortunate travelers with time to explore the rich treasures of Florence and the spectacular surrounding countryside as well, innumerable surprises await them. On the extreme outskirts of the city, the Fattoressa offers the ideal location for this type of "dual" exploration. One of the many marvelous attractions of Florence is how the countryside comes right up to the doors of the city. Just behind the magnificent Certosa monastery is situated the 15th-century stone farmhouse of the delightfully congenial Fusi-Borgioli family. With loving care, they have transformed the farmer's quarters into guest accommodations: four sweetly simple bedrooms, each with its own spotless bathroom. Angiolina and Amelio, natural bed-and-breakfast hosts, treat their guests like family and, as a result, enjoy receiving some of them year after year. With the addition of two bedrooms daughter-in-law, Laura, who speaks English, has been a great help. Visitors take meals *en famille* at long tables in the cozy, rustic dining room with a large stone fireplace. Here Angiolina proudly serves authentic Florentine specialties using ingredients from her own fruit orchard and vegetable garden. *Directions:* Entering Florence from the Certosa exit off the Siena superstrada, turn left one street after the Certosa Convent. After the bridge, turn right behind the building (Via Volterrana—slightly hidden). The house is just on the left.

LA FATTORESSA
Hosts: Angiolina Fusi & Amelio Borgioli
Via Volterrana 58
Galluzzo (FI) 50124, Italy
Tel & fax: (055) 2048418
6 rooms with private bathrooms
Lire 120,000–140,000 double B&B
Breakfast and dinner served
Open all year
Some English spoken
Region: Tuscany

A very pleasant alternative to hotels in Florence is a stay at the Milione wine estate in the hills overlooking the city. Jessica Brandimarte oversees this expansive farm property with its large olive oil and wine production as well as a successful silver-making operation, the pride of her late husband. All the sculptures seen on the property are his own creations. Many rooms and apartments are divided among the main villa and another complex of stone farmhouses a short distance down the road. They are well decorated with lovely country antiques, terra-cotta brick floors, beamed ceilings, and dried flower bouquets. Each room varies in size and decor, many are equipped with kitchenette and eating area. Most have wonderful views over the soft hills lined with vineyards. The swimming pool is surrounded by flower-filled terra-cotta vases and bordered by a wood-paneled house with changing rooms for the convenience of guests. Fresh bread and homemade jam are provided for breakfast daily in all rooms. Dinner is served upon request, and is taken together around one long table. *Directions:* Exit from the autostrada at Certosa. Follow signs for Firenze city center and turn left at Galluzzo. Follow the road for 2 kilometers and turn a sharp right at the sign for Rossi Ristorante.

IL MILIONE
Hosts: Brandimarte family
Via di Giogoli 14
Florence 50124, Italy
Tel: (055) 2048713
4 rooms with private bathrooms
5 apartments
Lire 120,000 double B&B
3-day minimum stay
All meals served
Open all year
English spoken well
Region: Tuscany

The Casa Nova bed and breakfast, in relation to our other more remote selections in the area, has the advantage of being on the edge of Greve, the center of the Chianti region. Although right next to the newer section of town, the large hilly property covered with vineyards seems deep in the countryside. Any new construction is absolutely invisible from the house. Sandra Taccetti and her husband offer their stone farmhouse with six bedrooms for guests, while they live in the converted barn. There is a simple and casual feel to the place and guests can be right at home in the downstairs living room with its floral-print sofas, breakfast room, or out on the back porch overlooking the garden and lush green landscape. The clean and uncluttered bedrooms, all with bathrooms except one, are appropriately decorated with country antiques. The beamed ceilings and brick floors naturally make up the rest of the decor. The two adjoining rooms with shared bathroom are ideal for a family of four, while two other doubles each have their own terrace. From Casa Nova you are equidistant to Florence and Siena. *Directions:* From Florence coming into town, turn left at the first stoplight, Via Gramsci, and follow the curve up to the left. The road ends at the house. *Note:* Via di Uzzano has nothing to do with signs for Castello di Uzzano.

CASA NOVA
Hostess: Sandra Taccetti
Via di Uzzano 30
Greve in Chianti (FI) 50022, Italy
Tel & fax: (055) 853459
6 rooms, 5 with private bathrooms
Lire 110,000 double B&B
Breakfast only
Open all year
Very little English spoken
Region: Tuscany

LE VALLI (INCISA VAL D'ARNO) SAN NICCOLO D'OLMETO Map: 8b

Just 18 kilometers from Florence, tucked away on a hilltop in Chianti, is the marvelous convent of San Niccolo d'Olmeto with its medieval tower, Romanesque church, and Renaissance cloister. The Cavagnari family, with their architecture and hotelier background (they are owners of the J & J Hotel in the center of Florence), took on the very ambitious task of restoring the dilapidated buildings to their original beauty. The peaceful and enchanting setting with its surrounding woods, vineyards, and olive groves makes this a perfect spot for dreamers. The main villa is a showcase for the family's antique and art collection which blends in effectively with more modern light fixtures and furniture. Clever architectural tricks are incorporated to create divisions between rooms, arched doorways, and a bridge in the tower. Every little window has gorgeous views of the countryside. In another wing of the complex are the five spacious suites for two to four persons, decorated comfortably with more fine antique pieces. These are rented out by the week and include their own equipped kitchenette. An added plus is the swimming pool beside the rose garden. (Reservations are made through the hotel.) *Directions:* Exit at Incisa from A1 autostrada and head north on route 69. Pass Burchio and watch for a small yellow sign on the left.

SAN NICCOLO D'OLMETO
Hosts: Cavagnari family
Localita: Le Valli
Incisa Val d'Arno (FI) 50066, Italy
Tel: (055) 240951 Fax: (055) 240282
5 suites for weekly rental
Lire 1,200,000–1,500,000 weekly
Breakfast and dinner upon request
Open April to October
English spoken very well
Region: Tuscany

An outstanding alternative to the city hotels of Venice is the perfectly charming Gargan bed and breakfast situated in the countryside just 30 kilometers from Venice. The Calzavara family renovated the family's expansive 17th-century country house and opened the restaurant and guestrooms just five years ago, offering four sweetly decorated bedrooms each with its own bathroom on the top floor plus two suites consisting of two bedrooms and one bathroom. Signora Calzavara enjoys making her guests feel as "at home" as possible by having fresh flowers in the cozy, antique-filled bedrooms. The downstairs sitting and dining rooms display the family's country antiques as well as a large fireplace and nice touches such as lace curtains and paintings. Guests are treated to a full breakfast of homebaked cakes and exceptional five-course dinners prepared by Renzia, a renowned chef of Treviso with her own cooking school, using all ingredients from their farm. The Gargan is an ideal choice in this area, being a short drive from such marvels as Padova, Venice, Treviso, Vicenza, Verona, and Palladian Villas plus many smaller medieval villages. *Directions:* From Venice take route 245 to Scorze then follow signposts to S. Ambragio, taking a left at the stoplight after town. Follow the road for 1 kilometer to Levada. There is a local train from Padova.

GARGAN
Hosts: Calzavara family
Via Marco Polo 2
Levada di Piombino Dese (PD) 35017, Italy
Tel: (049) 9350308
4 rooms, 2 suites, all with private bathrooms
Lire 90,000 double B&B
  87,000 per person half board
All meals served
Open all year
Some English spoken
Region: Veneto

In the remote, rugged backhills of Chianti countryside, on the highest peak of Monte San Michele, is a cluster of stone houses dating from 1300 that has been gradually restored according to original drawings. Stefano and Patrizia, the Florentine hosts as of two years, offer warm hospitality and excellent Tuscan fare such as torciglioni and pappardelle pasta dishes, Florentine steak, and variations on wild boar. Patrizia works magic in the kitchen while husband Stefano entertains guests in the two intimate dining rooms. During the warmer months, regulars request the outdoor terrace with grape arbor overlooking the brilliant green landscape. There are four bedrooms available to guests, one having an en-suite bathroom, and another two with communicating rooms sharing one bathroom, perfect for a family of four. The rooms are simply but tastefully appointed with antique armoires and colorful bedspreads. A locanda, being traditionally a restaurant informally offering a bed to weary overnight travelers, puts emphasis on the evening meal rather than breakfast, so one must stop in town for a coffee before starting the day. *Directions*: Take the Incisa exit off the Florence–Siena highway, following signs for Greve. After 14 kilometers (Greve is 10 kilometers beyond) turn left for Lucolena/Monte San Michele, and follow the road up the mountain for 7 kilometers.

LOCANDA BORGO ANTICO
Hosts: Patrizia Betti & Stefano Fissi
Localita: Lucolena, Via Case Sparse 115
Greve in Chianti (FI) 50020, Italy
Tel: (055) 851024
4 rooms, 3 with private bathrooms
Lire 90,000 double
Lunch and dinner served (closed Tuesdays)
Open March to October
Credit cards: MC, VS
Very little English spoken
Region: Tuscany

Just south of the fascinating Etruscan/medieval villages of Montemerano, Sovana, and Saturnia (well-known for the 2,000-year-old hot springs), this isolated bed and breakfast is situated within a national park. A cluster of stone buildings, neglected for decades, was once a community serving the castle down the road. This is where two extraordinarily determined Dutch women decided to settle, and the results of their renovating efforts are truly miraculous. Six guestrooms have been tastefully fashioned in one part of the sectioned farmhouse, each with its own distinct personality and color scheme. Special marbling techniques have been applied to the walls in warm earth tones, lending an intimate feeling to the rooms. Antique furniture mixes well with wicker pieces, enhanced by the rich terra-cotta floors and beamed ceilings. A minor dilemma of how to make a windowless passageway appealing was resolved by importing an Austrian surrealistic painter to fresco the walls, floor, and ceiling. The trompe l'oeil effect is like walking onto a terrace on a romantic starry night. Other amenities include a cozy kitchen and a library for guests. In the vicinity are horse stables and a golf course. *Directions:* From Rome (1-1/2 hours away), take the Aurelia road to Vulci, then follow signs for Manciano. Campigliola is on the left, 9 kilometers before town.

CAMPIGLIOLA COUNTRY CLUB
Hosts: Frida Van der Horst & P. J. Van den Bergh
Localita: Campigliola, Manciano (GR) 58014, Italy
Tel & fax: (0564) 629194
6 rooms with private bathrooms
Lire 132,000 double B&B
2-day minimum stay
Breakfast only
Open all year
Credit cards: VS
English spoken well
Region: Tuscany

We are delighted to include the newly opened La Biancarda bed and breakfast, the lovely country home of the Florio family of Ancona, in the heart of the Conero National Park. Just south of Ancona begins one of the prettiest coastlines of the eastern side with a combination of seaside villages, hilly countryside, and dramatic mountains cascading into the sea. Signora Giovanna had the salmon-colored farmhouse dating to 1760 restored eight years ago to provide her family with a relaxing country retreat, and adorned it with many of the family's precious antiques. The stone-walled living room with enormous fireplace, cozy library, and billiard room are all open to guests. Six guest bedrooms include a suite with living room. A real treat is waking up to breakfast in the delightful country kitchen with fireplace, long family table, beamed ceilings, and collection of hanging brass pots. Dinner based on fresh fish and local produce and wines can also be arranged. Outdoor activities in the area include golf, tennis, horseback riding, and swimming (beaches are ten minutes away). *Directions*: From the A14 autostrada exit at Ancona Sud and follow signs for Camerano then Poggio where you turn right on the coastal road. After 4 kilometers turn right for Massignano and call from town.

LA BIANCARDA   **NEW**
Hosts: Giovanna Florio & family
Via Biancarda 129
Massignano (AN) 60125, Italy
Tel & fax: (071) 2800503 or 34331
Tel (off-season): (071) 203219
6 bedrooms, 5 with private bathrooms
Lire 160,000–220,000 double B&B
2-day minimum stay
Breakfast, dinner upon request
Open May to October 15
English spoken well
Region: Marches

The very simple but economical Oasi Verde or "green oasis" is just that; a convenient roadside stop for those traveling between Umbria and the Marches region. Carla and Andrea Rossi inherited the sprawling 200-year-old stone farmhouse and surrounding land, ideally located midway between Perugia and Gubbio (a not-to-be-missed medieval stone village set high up in the hillside), and decided to convert it to a bed and breakfast and restaurant. The eight rooms, each with own bathroom, have been decorated like model room number 3, with its original beamed ceiling and country-antique bed and armoire. White-tiled floors may be out of character, but give a sense of cleanliness nonetheless. Another wing of the complex houses three simply furnished apartments for longer stays, perfect for a family of four. The windows at the back of the house open out to green hills with alternating patches of woods and sunflower fields. The facilities have recently been enhanced by the addition of a swimming pool and bikes available for rent. *Directions:* From Perugia on route 298 after 25 kilometers, you find the bed and breakfast on the left-hand side, at Mengara, 10 kilometers before reaching Gubbio.

OASI VERDE
Hosts: Andrea & Carla Rossi
Localita: Mengara 1
Gubbio (PG) 06024, Italy
Tel: (075) 920156 Fax: (075) 920049
8 rooms with private bathrooms, 3 apartments
Lire 85,000 double B&B
* 70,000 per person half board*
3-day minimum stay (high season)
All meals served
Open all year
Credit cards: MC, VS
Very little English spoken
Region: Umbria

Florentine sisters Francesca and Beatrice Baccetti eagerly accepted the challenge of converting the family's country home and vineyards into a bed and breakfast. Restoration work began immediately on the two adjacent stone buildings dating back to 1400. All original architectural features were preserved, leaving the five guestrooms and ten apartments (for two to four people) with clay-tiled floors, wood-beamed ceilings, mansard roofs, and generous views over the tranquil Tuscan countryside. The very comfortable and tidy rooms are furnished with good reproductions and feel almost hotel-like, with telephone, television, and modern bathrooms in each. A beautiful swimming pool with hydro-massage, tennis courts, billiards room, and nearby horse stables are at the guests' disposal, although finding enough to do is hardly a problem with Florence only 18 kilometers away and practically all of Tuscany at one's fingertips. Breakfast is served at wood tables in the stone-walled dining room or out on the terrace. Readers give Salvadonica a high rating. Directions: From Florence take the superstrada toward Siena for 20 kilometers, exiting at San Casciano Nord. Follow signs for town, turning left at the sign for Mercatale. Salvadonica is on this road and well marked.

SALVADONICA
Hosts: Francesca & Beatrice Baccetti
Via Grevigiana 82
Mercatale Val di Pesa (FI) 50024, Italy
Tel: (055) 8218039 Fax: (055) 8218043
5 rooms with private bathrooms, 10 apartments
Lire 130,000–150,000 double B&B
3-day minimum stay, 1 week high season
Breakfast only
Open March to October
Credit cards: all major
English spoken very well
Region: Tuscany

In a city where the word "charm" is practically non-existent, the Hotel Regina came as a pleasant surprise among the rather nondescript choice of modern hotels in the city. For those flying in and out of Milan, with a desire to catch a glimpse of the city center, this is an ideal selection. The attractive, typically 18th-century façade and entrance invite guests into a luminous reception area converted from the original courtyard with stone columns, arches, marble floors, and a small corner bar. Completely refurbished rooms include all modern amenities and are very quiet, being set off the street. Decorated comfortably and uniformly with identical furniture, warmth is given to rooms with soft pastel-colored walls, parquet floors, and scattered Oriental rugs. A full buffet breakfast is served below and is included in the room rate. Linate airport is easily reached by cab in 20 minutes, while the Malpensa airport can be reached by bus from the train station. *Directions*: Via Correnti is just off the Via Torino which leads to Milan's famous cathedral and shopping area, and is between the Basilicas of San Lorenzo and San Ambrogio.

HOTEL REGINA   **NEW**
Host: Signor Doragrossa
Via Cesare Correnti 13
Milan 20123, Italy
Tel: (02) 58106913 Fax: (02) 58107033
43 rooms with private bathrooms
Lire 250,000–340,000 double B&B
Breakfast only
Open all year
Credit cards: all major
Some English spoken
Region: Lombardy

Just 20 kilometers from Siena, at the foot of Chianti is the Godiolo stone farmhouse with its double loggia and cupola dating back to 1350. Red geraniums cascade from every one of the balconies and terra-cotta urns. While Signor Giuliano tends to the vineyards and wine-production, Signora Bianca dedicates her time to making their guests feel very much at home. What used to be the children's rooms are now four charming guestrooms with nice touches—embroidered linen sheets and dried flower arrangements. Breakfast in the typical tiled kitchen consists of homemade baked goods to which guests help themselves. Signora, with her Roman-Tuscan origins, is an excellent cook and guests can treat themselves to a delightful dinner with the family. Their son, Stefano, when not studying, is often around to assist and is eager to practice his English. Nearby are the thermal baths of Rapolano where massages, mud baths, and other spa services are available—true relaxation. *Directions:* Exit from the A1 autostrada at Val di Chiana and head towards Siena on route 326 towards Serre di Rapolano, but turn right, up to Godiolo rather than left into town.

GODIOLO
Hosts: Giuliano & Bianca Perinelli
Localita: Modanella
Serre di Rapolano, (SI) 53040, Italy
Tel: (0577) 704304
4 rooms with private bathrooms
Lire 200,000 double B&B
Dinner served upon request
Open all year
Some English spoken
Region: Tuscany

On the same road as the Godiolo bed and breakfast, a more independent type of accommodation is offered at the 13th-century Castello di Modanella. It is a sprawling stone complex complete with towers and turrets, several separate houses where the farmers of the vast wine estate once lived, a church, and even a school. The castle is in a constant state of restoration and along the way 13 rental apartments have been incorporated in various sections. Some apartments can be found in the old schoolhouse on two floors with one, two, or three bedrooms, bathrooms, kitchen, and living room. They maintain a true rustic flavor with original beams, mansard ceilings, worn brick floors, stone walls, and a mix of old and new wood furniture. All have lovely views over the countryside. Five other comfortable apartments are located down the road within a separate house next to the swimming pool and tennis courts. Although currently there are no accommodations in the castle itself, it is worth a visit with its arched entrance, iron gates, stone courtyard, and clock tower. The estate is under the direction of Gabriella Cerretti who assists guests with their every need. *Directions:* Travel for 30 kilometers from Siena on route 326 towards the autostrada, then turn left at the sign for the Castello, opposite Serre di Rapolano.

CASTELLO DI MODANELLA
Hostess: Gabriella Cerretti
Serre di Rapolano (SI) 53040, Italy
Tel: (0577) 704604 Fax: (0577) 704740
13 apartments for 2 to 9 persons
Lire 170,00–350,000 daily
2-day minimum stay
No meals served
Open all year
Some English spoken
Region: Tuscany

While many agritourism farms are run by transplanted urbanites, many are still owned and operated by farmers whose families have worked the land for generations. Such is the case with Onofrio Contento and his family, proprietors of Masseria Curatori, not far from the city of Monopoli and the Adriatic Sea, where, for five generations, the family has produced olives, almonds, and cattle. Inside the main coral-color house are modest and immaculate quarters for guests, consisting presently of two two-bedroom apartments with kitchens, plus three doubles, one with private bath. Old and new family furniture has been combined to decorate the rooms. The view is pleasingly pastoral, overlooking olive-tree studded hills. Several new rooms have just been completed in a nearby building overlooking a lovely stone-walled garden and fruit orchard. Breakfast and extra meals are taken together with the family in their dining room. Horseback riding is also arranged for guests. This lodging is recommended for visitors with some command of the Italian language. *Directions:* 40 kilometers from Brindisi. Take coastal route N16, exiting at Monopoli-San Francesco da Paola. Take the road back across the highway and take the first left. Follow Via Conchia for 2 kilometers to the pink house.

MASSERIA CURATORI
Hosts: Onofrio Contento family
Contrada Cristo delle Zolle 227
Monopoli (BA) 70043, Italy
Tel: (080) 777472
6 rooms, 4 with private bathrooms, 2 apartments
Lire 60,000 double B&B
* 50,000 per person half board*
2-day minimum stay
All meals served
Open all year
Very little English spoken
Region: Apulia

The culturally rich region of Veneto, with its Palladio villas and enchanting towns such as Verona, Vicenza, and Padua, merits more than a cursory visit and will handsomely reward the effort. Just south of Padua, outside the medieval town of Monselice with its imposing castle, is the family-run bed and breakfast of Silvia Sagradin and family. Ten years ago they restored the late-19th-century farmhouse, converting the stables into a large airy restaurant equipped with long family-style wooden tables and copper pots hanging from the ceiling. The eatery has become a favorite Sunday outing for both rural and urban folk, largely due to the superior country cuisine served there. The entire family is involved in the effort, either as hosts, working in the fruit orchards, or on site in the busy kitchen, where it seems fresh pasta is being prepared at all hours. For guests wishing to stay overnight, two rooms have recently been incorporated into the house. Ideal for a family of four, this separate section of the house includes the two bedrooms (decorated with inherited country furniture, lace curtains, and beamed ceilings), newly built bathroom, and a small private dining area. *Directions:* Take the A13 autostrada south toward Ferrara, exiting at Monselice, then follow the yellow signs to Molini, 20 kilometers from Padua.

FATTORIA SAVELLON MOLINI
Hosts: Silvia Sagradin & family
Via Savellon Molini
Monselice (PD) 35042, Italy
Tel: (0429) 73135/782212
2 rooms sharing a bathroom
Lire 70,000 double B&B
 55,000 per person half board
All meals served
Open Easter to September
Very little English spoken
Region: Veneto

As you travel southwest toward Florence through the foothills of the Appenines, the scenery transforms itself dramatically from the flatlands of the *padana* into soft green hills textured with alternating fields of wheat and grape vines. From Bologna, the Tenuta Bonzara farm and vineyard is a half-hour drive up a road that winds through scented pine forest, arriving at a group of houses owned by several farming families. The wine estate is owned by Dottor Lambertini of Bologna, and is run by warm-hearted Mario and his family, whose main responsibility is overseeing the wine production. Guest accommodation on the estate consists of two small houses containing two apartments, each with one or two bedrooms, bathroom, kitchenette, and sitting room—the nicest are the one-bedroom apartments in the older house with small corner fireplaces, red-brick floors and beamed ceilings, rustically furnished with simple pinewood pieces. A trattoria on the premises serves meals, and a museum has been set up in the old barn displaying antique farm tools, carts, and agricultural machines. Horseback riding is available, and participation in the grape harvesting is encouraged. *Directions:* Take the Bologna/Casalecchio exit from the A1 autostrada and continue to Gesso, Rivabella, San Chierlo, and Monte San Pietro, where you go left up the hill.

TENUTA BONZARA
Host: Dottor Francesco Lambertini
Via San Chierlo 37
Monte San Pietro (BO) 40050, Italy
Tel: (051) 6768324 Fax: (051) 225772
4 apartments
Lire 600,000 weekly
3-day minimum stay in low season
Trattoria on premises (dinner only)
Open May to October
Some English spoken
Region: Emilia-Romagna

The scenic approach to the Fattoria di Vibio passes through lush green hills, by picturesque farms, and is highlighted by a romantic view of the quaint town of Todi, 20 kilometers away. Two handsome brothers from Rome run this top-drawer bed and breakfast consisting of several recently restored stone houses. The houses sit side by side and share between them ten double rooms with private baths. Common areas for guests include a cozy, country-style living room with fireplace, games room, and country kitchen. The accommodations are enhanced by preserved architectural features such as terra-cotta floors and exposed-beam ceilings, and typical Umbrian handicrafts such as wrought-iron beds, renovated antiques, and *Deruta* ceramics. On the assumption that guests may find it difficult to leave this haven, the hosts offer only half board, along with a beautiful swimming pool, tennis, hiking, horseback riding, and biking. Signora Gabriella, with a passion for cooking, gets all the richly deserved credit for the marvelous meals served either poolside or on the panoramic terrace. *Directions:* From either Todi or Orvieto follow route S448 until the turnoff for Vibio just outside Todi. Follow the well-marked dirt road for 10 kilometers.

FATTORIA DI VIBIO
Hosts: Giuseppe Saladini & Gabriella Moscati
Localita: Buchella-Doglio
San Venanzo (TR) 05010, Italy
Tel: (075) 8749607 Fax: (075) 8780014
10 rooms with private bathrooms
Lire 110,000 per person half board
3-day minimum stay. 1 week June 15 to Sep 15
Breakfast and dinner served
Open March to November
Credit cards: AX, VS
Very little English spoken
Region: Umbria

Surprisingly, one of the least visited regions in Italy is the Marches, an area rich in culture, nature, and history bordering on the Adriatic. Just 15 kilometers from the coast in the heart of this gentle, hilly countryside, is the Campana farm, run by 10 families of professionals and artists who came here from Milan in search of an alternative lifestyle. The farm, made up of four pale-peach stone houses dating from 1700, has been restored with great care and taste, making space for private quarters, a refined restaurant, wine cellar, studio, music room, and, for guests, two double rooms and an apartment with two bedrooms. The latter has lovely terraces looking across vineyard-covered hills to the distant sea, and are decorated with a combination of old and new furnishings. With the recent renovation of a separate two-story house on the property, four additional bedrooms are offered to guests. Drawing on the considerable pool of available talent, an unusual variety of activities is offered—from courses in painting, theater, sculpture, and photography to workshops in crafting leather, silk, and wool. A swimming pool and tennis courts were recently added. *Directions:* From Ancona go south on the A14 autostrada, exit at Pedaso and continue south to Carassai, then turn right. After 5 kilometers, turn right for Montefiore, then left at the small sign for La Campana.

LA CAMPANA
Hosts: Co-op Agricola
Via Menocchia 39
Montefiore d'Aso (AP) 63010, Italy
Tel: (0734) 938229 Fax: (0734) 938484
6 rooms and 1 apartment with private bathrooms
Lire 90,000–120,000 double B&B
60,000–90,000 per person half board
Breakfast and dinner served
Open all year
English spoken well
Region: Marches

La Loggia, built in 1427, was one of the Medici estates during the centuries they ruled over Florence and surrounding territories. Owner Giulio Baruffaldi, weary of urban life in Milan, transplanted himself and his wife here and succeeded in reviving the estate's splendor while respecting its past, enhancing its architectural beauty while giving utmost attention to comforts and warmth. Their informal yet refined hospitality is reflected in the care given to the decor of the apartment-suites, each containing one to three bedrooms, living room, kitchen, fireplace, and many lovely antiques and original paintings from the Baruffaldis' own art collection. In fact, many important bronze and ceramic sculptures by international artists are displayed throughout the gardens of the villa. Apart from just basking in the pure romance and tranquillity of this place, there is a swimming pool, horseback riding, and nearby tennis and golf facilities. Other activities include the occasional cooking or wine-tasting lesson, and impromptu dinners in the cellar. The hosts and their absolutely charming guest assistant, Ivana, seem to exist merely to pamper their guests' every whim. This is the stuff dreams are made of. *Directions:* From the Florence-Siena autostrada, exit after San Casciano at Bargino. Turn right at the end of the ramp, then left for Montefiridolfi (3.5 kilometers). La Loggia is just outside town.

FATTORIA LA LOGGIA
Hosts: Giulio Baruffaldi & Cuca Roaldi
Via Collina, Montefiridolfi in Chianti
San Casciano Val di Pesa (FI) 50020, Italy
Tel: (055) 8244288 Fax: (055) 8244283
10 apartments (for 2 to 7 persons)
Lire 250,000–450,000 per apartment daily
3-day minimum stay, weekly stay preferred
Breakfast and occasional dinner
Open all year
Fluent English spoken
Region: Tuscany

One result of increasing interest in the singular attractions of the *maremma*, or southern Tuscany, is the opening or expansion of several noteworthy places to stay. The Villa Acquaviva, once owned by nobility, has been a small family hotel for the past nine years. The ambitious proprietors, Serafino and Valentina, completed extensive remodeling to include seven guestrooms named for and painted in the colors of local wildflowers. The bedrooms all have private baths, and are decorated with country antiques and wrought-iron beds. The charming breakfast room has sky-blue tablecloths and looks out arched windows to a lush flower garden with alternating palms and umbrella pines, and on to a view over the gently rolling landscape up to the village of Montemerano—a quaint, medieval town with excellent restaurants and artisan shops. Breakfast of homemade cakes, breads, and jams can be taken inside or out on the patio. Just completed last year are eight additional rooms in a stone farmhouse on the property. These are our new favorites, with beautiful local antiques and colorful matching fabrics adorning beds and windows. The farmhouse has its own spacious breakfast room and living area downstairs. *Directions:* From Rome, take the Aurelia road, exiting at Vulci. Follow signs for Manciano, then for Montemerano. Approximately 1-1/2 hours from Rome.

VILLA ACQUAVIVA
Hosts: Valentina di Virginio & Serafino d'Ascenzi
Localita: Acquaviva
Montemerano (GR) 58050, Italy
Tel: (0564) 602890 Fax: (0564) 602895
15 rooms with private bathrooms
Lire 130,000 double B&B
3-day minimum stay in high season
Breakfast only
Closed February
English spoken well
Region: Tuscany

Another welcome addition to our bed and breakfast collection is the Fontanelle country house, sitting in the heart of the Maremma area of Tuscany. Besides being pleasant and well-run, it fills a need for the growing interest in this off-the-track destination. Signor Perna and his two lovely daughters, originally from Rome, searched and found this peaceful haven from the stress of city life, promptly transferring themselves and undertaking major restoration work. Looking over a soft green valley up to the nearby village of Montemerano, the stone farmhouse with its rusty red shutters offers two comfortable rooms with spotless private bathrooms. The converted barn houses the remaining five rooms. Sunlight pours into the front veranda-like breakfast room where coffee and cakes are taken together with other guests at one large table. The Pernas assist guests in planning local itineraries including visits to artisan workshops. With due notice, guests can find a wonderfully prepared dinner awaiting them under the ivy-covered pergola in the rose garden. *Directions:* From Rome, take the A12 autostrada. Continue north on Aurelia route 1, turning off at Vulci after Montalto. Follow signs for Manciano then Montemerano. Turn left at the bed-and-breakfast sign before town and follow the dirt road for 4 kilometers.

LE FONTANELLE
Hosts: Daniela & Cristina Perna
Localita: Poderi di Montemerano
Montemerano (GR) 58050, Italy
Tel: (0564) 602762
7 rooms with private bathrooms
Lire 120,000 double B&B
Breakfast and dinner upon request
Open all year
Some English spoken
Region: Tuscany

For four generations the Laudomia has been an immensely popular mealtime stop for day trippers in picturesque southern Tuscany, serving exquisite fresh-pasta dishes among other delicacies. It made sense for Clara Casolaro and her daughter, Roberta, to add guestrooms so that visitors could linger and also take full advantage of their warm hospitality, comfortable accommodations, and unspoiled scenery. Son, Gianluca, following tradition, is now also one of the staff. Rooms across the street from the restaurant all have private baths and are simply but tastefully decorated with scattered antiques and bright floral bedspreads. The rooms off the roadside are quieter and offer lovely views across the rolling olive-tree-dotted hills. It is a memorable treat to dine in an intimate corner of the restaurant filled with family antiques and artwork. A grape-arbor garden in back is a delightful spot to relax on a summer evening. In the vicinity are the thermal hot springs of Saturnia and many intriguing medieval towns, including Pitigliano, which seems carved out of the limestone cliff. *Directions:* From Rome, take the Aurelia road north, turning off at Vulci. Follow signs for Manciano, then Montemerano. From Siena, take the superstrada to Grosseto. Follow signs for Scansano, then Montemerano.

LOCANDA LAUDOMIA
Hosts: Clara Casolaro & family
Poderi di Montemerano (GR) 58050, Italy
Tel: (0564) 620062/620013
12 rooms, 8 with private bathrooms
Lire 115,000 double B&B
  90,000 per person half board
3-day minimum stay
All meals served
Open all year
No English spoken
Region: Tuscany

Lucia Ana Luhan, whose parents are from Italy, grew up in a family rich in Italian tradition. After years of living in California and running a restaurant and catering business, she and her family have moved over permanently to Villa Lucia, the 500-year-old stone farmhouse, now a bed and breakfast, which she bought on a whim while on holiday in Italy a few years ago. Son, Jason, assists with the general running of the place while Lucia is busy with her cooking school and Italian language courses. All of the seven rooms are decorated in a homey, comfortable way; nothing contrived, just naturally pleasing and in keeping with the rustic nature of the old stone farmhouse. Three lovely apartments in the former barn are also available. When the weather is mild, a bountiful breakfast is served outside on the terrace where guests congregate again in late afternoon to sip cool drinks and socialize. Lucia has an "open house" policy, with a homemade pot of soup always on the burner plus snacks of cheese and salami on hand when guests return in the afternoon. Guests can also enjoy a sumptuous dinner when requested in the morning. The famous spa town of Montecatini is just a six-minute drive down the hill. The inn offers a small swimming pool and cooking lessons. *Directions:* Exit from autostrada A11 at Montecatini and follow signs for Monsummano (52 kilometers west of Florence). Montevettolini is 3 kilometers southwest of here.

VILLA LUCIA
Hostess: Lucia Ann Luhan
Via dei Bronzodi 144
Montevettolini (PT) 51010, Italy
7 rooms, 6 with private bathrooms
3 apartments
Tel & fax: (0572) 628817
$150 (US) double B&B
Breakfast and dinner served upon request
Open April 15 to November 15
English spoken very well
Region: Tuscany

Novella and Laerte Piangatelli, delightful and gregarious hosts, have been welcoming guests into their home for over ten years, ever since they moved to Emilia-Romangna from the south. Having agricultural experience, they were able to set up a farm, tended by Laerte, while Novella, the town schoolteacher, oversees the kitchen. She is an excellent cook and guests return time and time again for her pasta, joining the family at the long wood table in their rustic dining room with its hanging brass pots and ox harnesses. Guest accommodations have been transferred recently from upstairs in the white 18th-century farmhouse to the horse stalls, which have been converted into seven double rooms with private baths. The rooms are immaculate, if rather plain with basic modern furnishings. Guests tend to their own rooms and are even apt to help clear the table in the very informal and *en famille* atmosphere promoted at Le Radici. The sea, just 15 kilometers away, can be seen in the distance, and several medieval towns and castles dot the hills in the surrounding countryside. A unique experience, best enjoyed if you speak some Italian. *Directions:* On route 9 from Rimini to Cesana, follow signs for Calisese and Montiano. Turn left at the Esso gas station for Le Radici, or call for assistance.

LE RADICI
Hosts: Novella & Laerte Piangatelli
Localita: Montenovo
Via Golano 808
Montiano (OF) 47020, Italy
Tel: (0547) 327001
7 rooms with private bathrooms
Lire 55,000 per person half board
Breakfast and dinner served
Open March to December
No English spoken
Region: Emilia-Romangna

In the northern Piedmont region, leading into the foothills of the Alps, is the peaceful countryside where Piercarlo Novarese, Il Mompolino's cordial host, decided to establish his inn and equestrian center. Run more like a small hotel, the sixteen guestrooms are divided between two mustard-color buildings. Each room has a private bath and balcony, and is complemented with rustic furnishings. The larger suites feature sitting rooms and are the nicest, furnished with the occasional antique. A large, open dining room serves breakfast, lunch, and dinner, and boasts delectable regional dishes skillfully prepared by local women. Il Mompolino makes an ideal stopover on the way to the Alps, the lake region, or Milan. It also provides an appealing spot to relax for a few days between more demanding tourist destinations. Sports activities abound, including horseback riding, tennis, swimming, and a gym with sauna. A variety of horseback-riding lessons is offered at the equestrian center, as are mounted excursions into the adjacent national park. Perhaps a good idea between bowls of pasta! *Directions:* Take the Carisio exit from the Milan-Turin A4 autostrada. From Carisio Mompolino is 7 kilometers and well marked.

IL MOMPOLINO
Host: Piercarlo Novarese
Localita: Mompolino
Mottalciata (VC) 13030, Italy
Tel & fax: (0161) 857667
16 rooms with private bathrooms
2 apartments
Lire 100,000 double B&B
All meals served
Open all year
Credit cards: all major
Very little English spoken
Region: Piedmont

In a beautiful, unspoiled area of northern Umbria between the enchanting towns of Gubbio, Citta del Castello, and Perugia, travelers are made to feel at home in the Berna family's hillside farmhouse on their 100-acre property. The area, rich in Renaissance art and architecture, has become an international artists' colony, with frequently organized music festivals and art exhibits. Three small stone houses clustered together make up the property, two for guests and one for Marisa and her family who come and go from their native city of Rome. Stone walls, terra-cotta floors, and beamed ceilings lend natural charm to the rooms, while lace curtains, handsome country antiques, floral sofas, and dried flower arrangements enhance the cozy ambiance. Beautifully tiled bathrooms, living area, and downsized country kitchen are found in both houses, which are available for weekly rental only. In addition to being a gracious hostess, Marisa is actively involved in the community's cultural affairs and is an invaluable resource for information about the region. She also conducts week-long combination tours of cooking classes and local sightseeing. *Directions:* From Perugia take route N3, exiting at Umbertide. Follow signs for Niccone and turn left in town towards Mercatale. Turn right up the hill after 3 kilometers, or better, call from town!

LA MARIDIANA
Hosts: Gianni Berna family
Localita: Niccone 173
Umbertide (PG) 06019, Italy
Tel & fax: (075) 9303234
2 houses for 4 persons
Lire 1,000,000–1,500,000 weekly
Occasional dinner served on request
Open all year
English spoken very well
Region: Umbria

The location of La Chiocciola bed and breakfast, minutes from the main tollway from Rome to Florence and on the border of the Lazio and Umbria regions, is ideal. Added bonuses are the warm hospitality, deliciously prepared regional meals, and lovely country-style bedrooms. Roberto and Maria Cristina from Rome bought the stone farmhouse dating back to 1400 several years ago and began restoration work while living in the newer house next door. The results of their efforts are four perfectly neat and spotless bedrooms in each of the two houses, a living room area for guests, and a large rustic dining room with outdoor veranda. Obvious care and attention has been put into the decorating of the bedrooms with wrought-iron canopy beds, crisp, white linen curtains, and botanical prints. The 50-acre property with fruit orchards and vineyards is part of the Tiber river valley and woods. There are bicycles and a swimming pool for guests' use. Innumerable day trips and itineraries of special interest are offered in the area of Umbria and Lazio. *Directions*: From Rome or Florence on the A1 autostrada, exit at Orte and turn immediately left, passing under the tollway. Go in the direction of Amelia and repass over the tollway, taking the first left towards Penna in Teverina. La Chiocciola is 5 kilometers along this road.

LA CHIOCCIOLA   **NEW**
Hosts: Roberto & Maria Cristina de Fonseca Pimentel
Localita: Seripola
Orte (VT) 01028, Italy
Tel & fax: (0761) 402734
8 rooms with private bathrooms
Lire 120,000 double B&B
* 90,000 per person half board*
All meals served
Open all year
English spoken well
Region: Lazio

It was a pleasure to find such an authentic family farm so close to Orvieto, a fascinating and popular tourist destination, famous for its magical cathedral. The cordial Belcapo family actually owns two adjacent farms on the outskirts overlooking the majestic town on its limestone perch. La Cacciata also commands a dramatic view of the rich Umbrian valley below. The 200-acre farm/vineyard, in competent Belcapo-family hands for five generations, produces top-rated *Orvieto Classico* on a large scale, as well as a red and a rosé wine. The primary turn-of-the-century villa and one small stone house are reserved for family residences, while four other houses scattered around the property have been remodeled to accommodate guests. In the 15 rooms, all but two with private bathrooms, care has been taken to preserve authentic architectural features and to select refined country antiques which blend harmoniously with them. An airy dining room overlooking the countryside and horse stables serves up sumptuous dinners. A swimming pool has just been added looking up to picturesque Orvieto, and horses are available for lessons or scenic outings. *Directions:* Exit from the autostrada at Orvieto and turn left at the first stoplight on Viale 1 Maggio; follow signs for Porano, then signs to La Cacciata.

FATTORIA LA CACCIATA
Hosts: Settimio Belcapo family
Localita: Canale, Via La Cacciata 6
Orvieto (TR) 05010, Italy
Tel: (0763) 92881/300892 Fax: (0763) 41373
15 rooms, 13 with private bathrooms
Lire 90,000 double B&B
* 70,000 per person half board*
All meals served
Open all year
Very little English spoken
Region: Umbria

A convenient stopover while heading either north or south along the main artery—A1 autostrada—is the Villa Ciconia inn. Located below the historical center of Orvieto, in the newer commercial outskirts, the property maintains its tranquil setting thanks to the fortress of trees protecting the 16th-century stone villa. The first floor includes reception area, breakfast room, and two large high-ceilinged dining rooms. These latter, with their somber grey-stone fireplaces, tapestries, heavy dark-wood beams, and subdued-color frescoes depicting allegorical motifs and landscapes, give the place a medieval castle's air. The nine bedrooms on the second floor, all with en-suite bathrooms, are appointed in appropriate style, with antique chests and wrought-iron beds and all the amenities of a three-star hotel. Most rooms are quiet and look out onto the woods behind the villa. There are also two enormous beamed sitting rooms on this floor for guests. The restaurant has a solid reputation for creating excellent Umbrian specialties. *Directions:* Exiting from the autostrada, turn right towards Orvieto and right again where marked Arezzo, Perugia, passing under the tollway. The Ciconia is just after the river on the left-hand side of the road.

VILLA CICONIA
Hosts: Petrangeli family
Via dei Tigli 69
Orvieto (TR) 05018, Italy
Tel: (0763) 92982 Fax: (0763) 90677
9 rooms with private bathrooms
Lire 190,000–210,000 double B&B
All meals served
Open all year
Credit cards: all major
English spoken well
Region: Umbria

Claudia Spatola does a superb job of running a bed and breakfast in the complex of stone houses known as Borgo Spante which dates back to the 15th century and has been in her family since 1752. Consisting of a main villa, connecting farmers' houses, chapel, barns, swimming pool, and garden, it is isolated in 500 acres of woods and hills, yet only 10 miles from Orvieto and not far from Assisi, Todi, and Perugia. Guests stay in a combination of rooms and apartments in the former farmers' quarters with their irregular-sized rooms, sloping worn-brick floors, and rustic country furnishings—very charming in its way. Authentically Umbrian meals, prepared by local women, are served in the dining room with long wood tables and fireplace. A larger dining area has been added in the former barn, along with four additional mini-apartments—simply and characteristically decorated. Memorable evenings are spent in the garden or poolside conversing with other guests or listening to an impromptu concert. *Directions:* From the A1 autostrada exit at Orvieto and follow signs for Arezzo on route 71. After 7 kilometers, turn right at Morrano and proceed for 12 kilometers to the sign for Spante. Turn left and continue for 2 kilometers.

BORGO SPANTE
Hostess: Claudia Spatola
Localita: Ospedaletto
San Venanzo (TR) 05010, Italy
Tel & fax: (075) 8709134/8709272
5 rooms with private bathrooms
8 apartments
Lire 90,000 per person half board
2-day minimum stay
Breakfast and dinner served
Open all year
Some English spoken
Region: Umbria

Lo Spagnulo gives us a good idea of how the *masseria* farms of Apulia functioned in the 1600s. They were self-sufficient agricultural production centers, described as "factories," which included the proprietor's villa, housing for farmers, common dining area, church, administrative offices, animal shelters, and work areas. The Spagnulo still cultivates animals, fresh produce, almonds, and olives. Fortress-like in appearance, its white-stone exterior leads inside to a courtyard garden, off which the guest quarters are located. These vary in size and shape, many comprising two or three bedrooms, living/eating area, and kitchen. Featuring the vaulted ceilings, exposed beams, terra-cotta floors and stone walls of the original building. The rooms display charm despite the somewhat spartan furnishings. These accommodations are recommended over the nondescript rooms which have been added in a modern building nearby. The stalls have been converted into a restaurant for guests serving typical local dishes family style. Proprietor Livino Massari, a professor, and his family are present on weekends and during the summer. *Directions:* Heading south on Route 379, exit at Marina di Ostuni. Follow signs to Rosa Marina, turning left at the sign for the farm.

MASSERIA LO SPAGNULO
Host: Livino Massari
Localita: Rosa Marina-Contrada Spagnulo
Ostuni (BR) 72017, Italy
Tel: (0831) 970209 Fax: (0831) 333756
25 apartments
Lire 85,000 double B&B
* 60,000 per person half board*
All meals served
Open all year
Credit cards: AX, VS
English spoken well
Region: Apulia

Paciano, situated on the border of Umbria and Tuscany, south of Lake Trasimeno, is an intriguing medieval village, perfectly intact, and recently named the most ideal village in Italy. Here father and son team Giuseppe and Luigi Buitoni, of the famous pasta producing family, decided to put to use their refined culinary skills. The old olive oil press, part of the family's 12th-century residence, now functions as a restaurant with summer garden and bed and breakfast accommodation upstairs. Seven lovely bedrooms are decorated in refined country style, each with its own color scheme noted in the rich fabrics of the bedspreads and curtains. The palazzo was meticulously restored preserving all original architectural features while adding an extra floor and converting arched doorways to closets. The breakfast and sitting room is soft and inviting with splendid antiques, floral tapestry armchairs, fresh flowers, and crystal bottles lining shelves. A full buffet breakfast is served. Caterina, Luigi's darling bride, now helps welcome guests to the home. A part of the family's residence in the attached medieval tower is rented weekly—a special treat for a group of eight. *Directions:* Exit at Chiusi-Chianciano from the A1 autostrada; take the road towards Trasimeno and Perugia and turn right up to the town of Paciano where indicated.

LOCANDA DELLA ROCCA
Hosts: Buitoni family
Viale Roma 4
Paciano (PG) 06060, Italy
Tel: (075) 830236 Fax: (075) 830155
7 rooms with private bathrooms, 1 apartment
Lire 150,000 double B&B
All meals served
Credit cards: MC, VS
Open: March to December
English spoken well
Region: Umbria

The southernmost, "heel-side" of Italy's boot-shaped peninsula, known as *Puglia*, presents another facet of the country's many-sided culture. It is a land with spectacular coastlines, villages with distinct Greek and Turkish influence, endless lines of olive groves, fields of wild flowers, and a rich history of art including Pugliese Romanesque and baroque (Bari's Santa Nicola church is one of the most beautiful in Italy). All of this plus exquisite cuisine and a warm and open people await in *Puglia* (Apulia), as does the Masseria Salamina, a 16th-century fortified farmhouse between Bari and Brindisi covering 100 acres of land and producing primarily olive oil. The driveway leads to the sand-colored castle with turreted tower with expansive vistas sweeping to the sea. The seven suites, each with a separate entrance and freshly decorated with reproductions and wicker furniture, are found through the courtyard. Host Gianvincenzo and family live in the main wing and run their masseria with hotel efficiency and service. A large lofty restaurant with terra-cotta floors provides all meals for guests. Eight additional apartments are now available for longer stays. *Directions*: From the SS16 exit at Pezze di Greco. Just before town take the first right and follow it for 1 kilometer to the masseria.

MASSERIA SALAMINA
Host: Gianvincenzo De Miccolis Angelini
Pezze di Greco (BR) 72010, Italy
Tel & fax: (080) 727307/728582
7 suites with private bathrooms, 8 apartments
Lire 100,000–140,000 double B&B
 80,000–100,000 per person half board
1-week minimum stay in July & August
All meals served
Open all year
Credit cards: MC, VS
Some English spoken
Region: Apulia

Lovers of Tuscany's romantic countryside will envy the McCobbs, who after years in Rome decided to buy and restore an old stone farmhouse south of Siena and make a new home there. On the approach, at the crest of the dramatic cypress-lined drive, the visitor is rewarded with a 360-degree view of the soft, green hills dotted with villages. The panorama should be appreciated upon arrival as you'll likely have trouble tearing yourself away from the luxurious comfort of the spacious guest quarters and refreshing swimming pool. The four suites consist of a cozy sitting area, fireplace, writing desk, library, and amenities such as refrigerator, phone, and complimentary wine. The decor is a harmonious mix of antiques and family memorabilia (acquired through their world travels) which blend perfectly with the pretty floral-chintz upholstery and color-coordinated sheets. The palatial bathrooms are worth special mention since they provide so many decadent extras: whirlpool bath, his/her marble sinks, bathrobes, and plush towels. Fresh muffins and breads are served either in the atrium breakfast room or out on the terrace. *Directions:* From Rome take the A1 autostrada, exiting at Chiusi. After Montepulciano, follow signs for Pienza. After 6 kilometers watch for a small sign on the left indicating La Saracina.

LA SARACINA
Hosts: Jessie & Don McCobb
Strada Statale 146, km 29.7
Pienza (SI) 53026, Italy
Tel & fax: (0578) 748022
1 room, 4 suites, all with private bathrooms
Lire 230,000–320,000 double B&B
Breakfast only
Open all year, weekends only January to February
Credit cards: all major
Fluent English spoken
Region: Tuscany

Forty-five kilometers northeast of Florence, in a beautiful, hilly area of Tuscany, lies the Rufina valley, famous for its robust red wine. Crowning a wooded slope is one of the many residences of the noble Galeotti-Ottieri family. The 15th-century main villa, where the family lives when not in Florence, was once a convent. The interior reveals spacious high-ceilinged halls with frescoes depicting family history. The family has also restored several stone farmhouses on the vast property, one of which is the Locanda Praticino, whose upper floor contains eight lovely and simple double rooms, each with private bath and named after the color scheme they display. Downstairs is found a large dining and living room with vaulted ceiling, enormous stone fireplace, and family antiques. A unique loft bedroom in the third-floor cupola offers a sweeping view of the lush countryside. The addition of a swimming pool and tennis courts, plus enchanting landscape, makes it difficult to tear oneself away for touring. Available for longer stays are five very tastefully decorated apartments (two in the main house). The Petrognano is a tranquil spot where guests may enjoy the gracious hospitality of this historically important Florentine family. *Directions:* From Florence head toward Pontassieve. Continue to Rufina, turning right at Castiglioni-Pomino. The farm is just before Pomino.

FATTORIA PETROGNANO
Hostess: Cecilia Galeotti-Ottieri
Localita: Pomino
Rufina (FI) 50060, Italy
Tel: (055) 8318812 or 8318867
Fax: (055) 242918
8 rooms with private bathrooms
5 apartments
Lire 95,000 double B&B
All meals served
Open March to October
Little English spoken
Region: Tuscany

Elena and Cesare Taticchi heartily welcome guests to their tobacco and horse-breeding farm, a rambling Renaissance villa, above Perugia. The former stables near the main house contain a breakfast room and eight guestrooms with wood-beamed ceilings and brick floors, sweetly furnished in simple country style. Ceramic bathroom tile (and lamps), handmade by their talented daughter, depict horses, ducks, roses, butterflies, and the like, for which the rooms are named. The main villa's dramatic entrance foyer with arched stairway leads up to a glassed-in veranda overlooking a lush flower garden and woods through which the River Tiber flows. Elena serves her specialties in the elegant old-style dining room with chandelier and frescoes. Time stands still in the cluttered library/billiard room and the two living rooms with grand piano, Oriental carpets, and period paintings. Twenty horses are available for lessons in the indoor/outdoor ring or excursions in the area. Week-long courses with special all-inclusive rates are now available in cooking, ceramics, and riding. *Directions:* Take route E45 from Perugia and exit at Ponte Pattoli. Turn right at the T intersection and continue for 1 kilometer. The farm is just after the tennis/sport complex.

IL COVONE
Hosts: Elena & Cesare Taticchi
Strada della Fratticiola 2
Ponte Pattoli (PG) 06085, Italy
Tel: (075) 694140 Fax: (075) 694503
8 rooms, 6 with private bathrooms
Lire 120,000 double B&B (3-day minimum stay)
  95,000–115,000 per person half board
Breakfast and dinner served
Open all year
Credit cards: all major
Very little English spoken
Region: Umbria

Among the many islands off Italy, Ponza, just off the coast between Rome and Naples, has been a well-kept secret of Romans who frequent it primarily on summer weekends, thus retaining its authentic character as a fisherman's village. Most of the islanders live in the port area while the rest of the island is quite wild. Here you see a different aspect of Italian life while dining on divine fresh seafood and exploring the many coves and bays of inviting turquoise waters in a rented wooden *gozzo* (boat). The Sertoli family from Rome offers special accommodation in one of the original whitewashed houses on the hill above the port. On two levels, the compact main house, with long front shaded terrace looking out to sea, contains a living room, kitchen, and a double and a twin bedroom, each with its own bathroom just outside. They are comfortably appointed in simple seaside-home style with decorative blue-and-white tiled floors throughout. The third bedroom with bathroom is steps away in a separate little structure. Dinner can be arranged and is prepared and served at a neighbor's house—all delightfully informal and relaxing. It is a ten-minute walk to the beach and shops and restaurants in town. *Directions*: Take the car ferry or hydrofoil (one-hour trip) from Anzio (one hour south of Rome) or Circeo to Ponza port. With prior notice, taxi pick-up at the launch will be arranged.

I DUE PINI **NEW**
Hosts: The Sertoli family
Localita: Pizzicato
Isola di Ponza (LT) 04027, Italy
Tel & fax: (06) 3052537
3 bedrooms with private bathrooms
Lire 150,000 double B&B
  115,000 per person half board
3-day minimum stay
Breakfast and dinner served
Open May to October
English spoken well
Region: Lazio

The Vecchio Convento is a real gem, offering quality accommodation for a moderate price. Its several dining rooms are brimming with rustic country charm and serve delicious meals prepared from local produce. There are 20 guestrooms tastefully decorated with antiques—most have private bathrooms. The town of Portico di Romagna is like the inn, inviting yet unpretentious—an old village surrounded by wooded hills and clear mountain streams. A stroll through medieval pathways which twist down between the weathered stone houses leads you to an ancient stone bridge gracefully arching over a rushing stream. The inn, too, is old, but was not (as you might expect from its name) originally a convent. According to its gracious owner, Marisa Raggi, it was named for a restaurant located in a convent that she and her husband, Giovanni (the chef) used to operate—when they moved here they kept the original name. The restaurant (closed Wednesdays) is still their primary focus, as its fine, fresh cuisine reflects. Because of the winding, two-lane mountain highway which leads to the village, it takes about two hours to drive the 75 kilometers from Florence. *Directions:* The inn is located 34 kilometers southwest of the town of Forli.

ALBERGO AL VECCHIO CONVENTO
Hosts: Marisa Raggi & Giovanni Cameli
Via Roma 7
Portico di Romagna (FO) 47010, Italy
Tel: (0543) 967053 Fax: (0543) 967157
20 rooms, 15 with private bathrooms
Lire 134,000 double B&B
All meals served (except Wednesdays)
Open all year
Credit cards: all major
Some English spoken
Region: Emilia-Romagna

On the outskirts of historical Mantua sits the Villa Schiarino, one of the magnificent estates formerly belonging to the Gonzaga family, once among the most powerful nobility in Lombardy. The cordial Lena Eliseo family, the present owners, have taken on the enormous task of restoring the 15th-century palace room by room. With high vaulted ceilings, completely frescoed rooms, wrought-iron chandeliers, and original terra-cotta floors, the seemingly endless parade of rooms reveals one delight after another. Besides being a museum, the villa is also used for large parties, weddings, and business affairs. Surrounding the villa are small houses, once inhabited by farm hands, which are now available to travelers on a daily or weekly basis. The three modest but spacious and comfortable apartments are appointed with a mixture of antique and contemporary furniture and can accommodate up to four persons. Each apartment has its own living area and one includes a kitchenette. This location is the ideal spot to base yourself while exploring less-touristy Ferrara, Cremona, Verona, and Mantua, which are filled with medieval and Renaissance buildings (Palazzo del Te and Palazzo Ducale are "must-sees"). *Directions:* From Mantua take route N62 past the church and turn left on Via Gramsci. Follow it for 1 kilometer to the villa.

VILLA SCHIARINO LENA
Hosts: Lena Eliseo family
Via Santa Maddalena 7
Porto Mantovano (MN) 46047, Italy
Tel: (0376) 398238
3 apartments for 2 to 4 persons
Lire 90,000–120,000 daily per apartment
No meals served
Open all year
English spoken well
Region: Lombardy

High above the strip of shore holding the Fortino Napoleonico hotel sits the Hotel Emilia, owned by the Fiorini Dubbini family. Grandmother Emilia opened a small restaurant right on the beach 40 years ago, gaining an excellent reputation for fresh seafood dishes. That successful undertaking was followed by the hotel which, not surprisingly, has a restaurant known for seafood. It is surrounded by an extensive lawn sweeping to the edge of a cliff which drops 150 meters straight down to the sea below. Truly breathtaking views of Mount Conero and the dramatic, rugged coast can be enjoyed from this point as well as from any of the guestrooms. The hotel itself is rather stark and modern, with interiors softened by wicker couches topped by plump, yellow floral-print pillows, paintings, and flower bouquets. The all-white rooms are basic but comfortable, with wicker and rattan beds and clean, tiled bathrooms. This is a summer resort with swimming pool and tennis available on the premises, plus a nearby golf course. The cuisine, friendly hospitality, and unforgettable panoramas compensate for the somewhat spartan decor. *Directions:* Exit at Ancona Sud off autostrada A14 and follow signs for Camerano, then Portonovo. Watch for signs indicating the hotel's entrance.

HOTEL EMILIA
Hosts: Maurizio Fiorini family
Localita: Collina di Portonovo
Portonovo (AN) 60020, Italy
Tel: (071) 801145 Fax: (071) 801330
31 rooms with private bathrooms
6 apartments
Lire 150,000–200,000 double B&B
All meals served
Open all year
Credit cards: all major
English spoken well
Region: Marches

For those travelers wishing to explore the lesser-known Marches region, or about to embark on a ferry to Greece, the unique Fortino hotel offers comfortable and relaxing accommodations. Five kilometers along the coast from the city of Ancona, the hotel boasts a beachfront location. Originally a fortress, the vantage point it affords must have been considered strategic by Napoleon in 1811, when he ordered it constructed. Fifteen guestrooms, four suites, and a restaurant are housed within the low white, stone structure while the remaining 15 rooms are in a new building nearby. The restaurant specializes in fresh seafood dishes and looks so directly out to sea, it gives the impression of being on a ship. At the heart of the fort is a courtyard, complete with cannons, where breakfast is served, and a separate building contains a bar and a spacious living room with fireplace, decorated in neoclassic style. Rich period antiques appoint the three lovely suites, while simpler wicker furniture is found in the double rooms. Just two steps away is the beach, and up on the roof of the one-story fort is a deck with a spectacular coastal view. A swimming pool is also available for guests. *Directions:* From Ancona, follow signs for Camerano. Take a left at Portonovo, heading down to the sea. Watch for signs indicating the hotel's entrance.

FORTINO NAPOLEONICO
Hosts: Amleto Roscioni family
Via Poggio
Portonovo (AN) 60020, Italy
Tel: (071) 801450 Fax: (071) 801454
30 rooms and 4 suites with private bathrooms
Lire 230,000 double B&B
All meals served
Open all year
Credit cards: all major
English spoken well
Region: Marches

Accommodation of all levels is available in Positano's many hotels: from five-star luxury to simple bed and breakfasts. Casa Cosenza, with its sunny yellow façade, fits into the latter category. Sitting snug against the cliff side, halfway down to the beach, it is reached by descending one of the variety of stairways found in this unique seaside town. The front arched entranceway, lined with terra-cotta pots overflowing with colorful local flora, leads to an enormous tiled terrace overlooking the pastel-color houses of Positano and the dramatic coastline. Seven guestrooms on the second floor, each with private bathroom, enjoy the same breathtaking panorama. The residence dates back 200 years, as evidenced by the typical cupola ceilings in each room, originally designed to keep rooms cool and airy. Rooms have bright, tiled floors and are simply and sweetly decorated with old-fashioned armoires, desks, and beds. Room 7, although smaller and with an older bathroom, has a lovely large terrace, as does Room 2 which costs a little more. A Continental breakfast is served on the terrace. The helpful and very friendly Cosenza family assures visitors a pleasant stay. *Directions:* Park your car in a garage in town and ask for directions for the *scalinatella* stairway where there are signs to Casa Cosenza. Remember to pack light!

CASA COSENZA
Hosts: Cosenza family
Positano (SA) 84017, Italy
Tel: (089) 875063
7 rooms with private bathrooms, 2 apartments
Lire 120,000–160,000 double B&B
3-day minimum stay in high season
Breakfast only
Open all year
Very little English spoken
Region: Campania

There are few bed-and-breakfast-like accommodations along the spectacular Amalfi Coast, so the Fenice is a real find and as fantastic as the mythological bird for which it is named. Guests leave their cars on the main road and climb the arbored steps to discover the idyllic white villa hidden amid the lush Mediterranean vegetation. The incredibly hospitable young proprietors, Constantino and Angela, welcome new arrivals on the shady front terrace, where breakfast is served each clement morning, accompanied by classical music. Six spacious bedrooms, each with spotless bath and a terrace with wondrous sea views are situated in one wing of the family's antique-filled home. Seven more rooms with balconies, reached by *many* steps down from the road, are built separately into the side of the cliff and have colorful, tiled floors and similar furnishings. Descending yet *more* steps (always surrounded by incredible coastal views), you'll come across the curved sea-water pool and Jacuzzi carved against the rock, where a fresh Mediterranean lunch is served at one big table, prepared primarily with ingredients grown on the premises. This property is a natural wonder, cascading down to the sea and a small private beach. Our readers cannot seem to send us enough rave reviews about this place! *Directions:* Located on the coastal highway south of Positano in the direction of Amalfi, two curves after the town.

LA FENICE
Hosts: Angela & Constantino Mandara
Via Marconi 4
Positano (SA) 84017, Italy
Tel: (089) 875513
15 rooms with private bathrooms
Lire 160,000 double B&B
Breakfast and lunch served
Open all year
Very little English spoken
Region: Campania

The Villa Rucellai rates high among Italian bed and breakfasts, due to its setting, style, and gracious proprietors, the Rucellai Pique family. From the moment you enter the grand foyer looking out over the classical Italian Renaissance garden of this 16th-century country villa, all sense of time and place is lost. The Rucellais' devotion to their "farm" (in the family since 1759) is apparent, as is their warm and enthusiastic hospitality. Guests are given the run of the charming old home: from the cozy bedrooms, varying in size and decor, antique-filled library, and spacious living room with fireplace, plump floral sofas, and family portraits to the country kitchen and breakfast room overlooking a 14th-century pool, where guests are served *en famille* at a long wooden table. Members of the family enjoy suggesting itineraries of particular interest for their guests, as well as cultural events such as art courses, concerts, and art exhibits. The Villa Rucellai provides truly special accommodation as well as serving as an excellent base from which to visit Florence, Siena, Lucca, and Pisa. *Directions:* From Florence take the A11 autostrada, exiting at Prato Est. Turn right on Viale della Repubblica, then left on Borgo Valsugana, following signs for Trattoria La Fontana, and proceed on Via di Canneto for 2 kilometers up to the Villa.

VILLA RUCELLAI DI CANNETO
Hosts: Giovanna Rucellai Pique family
Via di Canneto 16
Prato (FI) 50047, Italy
Tel & fax: (0574) 460392
11 rooms, 9 with private bathrooms
Lire 140,000 double B&B
Breakfast only
Open all year
Fluent English spoken
Region: Tuscany

One option (among at least 20 possibilities) for in-home accommodations in the Radda area is at the home of a gregarious Florentine couple, Giuliana and Enis Vergelli, whose stone house sits on a long, winding road, just before the castle/village of Volpaia. The guest quarters are actually found in another stone house a few steps away in the quaint 14th-century village. The wood-shuttered residence can be rented entirely or as two separate apartments. One apartment is just like a doll house, comprised of a mini living area with minuscule fireplace, kitchenette, and a ladder staircase leading up to the bedroom and bath; an absolutely adorable love nest for two. The other apartment, also on two floors, has a good-sized living room with kitchen, bathroom, and two bedrooms, simply and very comfortably furnished. Giuliana also offers accommodation in a bedroom with bathroom and separate entrance in her home. Guests are welcome to wander through the Vergellis' garden and enjoy the terrace with sweeping views over Chianti country. Giuliana adores pampering her guests and appears now and then with jams, honey, or a freshly made soup. *Directions:* Driving through the town of Radda, turn right at signs for Volpaia castle. Follow uphill for several kilometers to the first house before entering town, marked Vergelli.

AZIENDA AGRICOLA VERGELLI
Hosts: Enis & Giuliana Vergelli
Localita: Volpaia
Radda in Chianti (SI) 53017, Italy
Tel: (0577) 738382
2 apartments, 1 room with private bathroom
$450 (US) weekly for 2 persons
$600 (US) weekly for 4 persons
Lire 80,000 double room
No meals served
Open all year
No English spoken
Region: Tuscany

Another addition to the group of house rentals in Radda is Le Selve, owned by a young couple who transferred to this serene countryside from Milan a few years ago. Their stone farmhouse is perched on a hilltop dominating the sweeping lush green landscape below—a truly heavenly 360-degree panorama. Sonia and Nando divided the house in three sections; one for themselves and their son, and two for their guests. The downstairs apartment has a bedroom, bathroom, and living room with kitchenette and eating area. Upstairs is a larger apartment with the same characteristics plus a terrace which enjoys the best view. Both are furnished very simply and have fully-equipped kitchens for independent travelers. Sonia's great passion for horses has her spending most of her time down at the stables, where outings in the gorgeous countryside are organized. A nice and quiet retreat, and a great base for exploring the scenic roads of Chianti. *Directions:* Coming from the west, just before Radda, turn right for San Sano and follow road until the sign S. Giusto in Salcio and turn right up hill to the farmhouse.

LE SELVE II
Hosts: Sonia & Nando Danieli
Localita: Le Selve-San Giusto
Radda in Chianti (SI) 53017, Italy
Tel: (0577) 738196
2 apartments
$450 (US) weekly for 2 persons
No meals served
Open all year
Some English spoken
Region: Tuscany

For its combination of idyllic location, charming ambiance, and delightful hosts, the Podere Terreno is an example of the best in Italian bed and breakfasts, with Sylvie and Roberto, a Franco-Italian couple, dedicating themselves to pampering their guests. The 400-year-old house is surrounded by terra-cotta flower vases, a grapevine-covered pergola, a small lake, and sweeping panoramas of the Chianti countryside. Within are seven sweet double bedrooms with bath, each decorated differently with country antiques and the family's personal possessions; a wine cellar loaded with the proprietors' own Chianti Classico; and a billiard room/library. Guests convene in the main room of the house around the massive stone fireplace on fluffy floral sofas for hors d'oeuvres before sitting down to a sumptuous candlelit dinner prepared by your hosts. This is a cozy, stone-walled room, filled with country antiques, brass pots and dried-flower bouquets hanging from the exposed beams, and shelves lined with bottles of wine— absolutely delightful. *Directions:* From Greve follow signs to Panzano, then go left for Radda and on to Lucarelli. After 3 kilometers turn right at Volpaia. After 5 kilometers, turn right at the sign for Podere Terreno.

PODERE TERRENO
Hosts: Marie Sylvie Haniez & Roberto Melosi
Via della Volpaia
Radda in Chianti (SI) 53017, Italy
Tel & fax: (0577) 738312
7 rooms with private bathrooms
Lire 120,000 per person half board
2-day minimum stay
Breakfast and dinner served
Open all year
Credit cards: MC, VS
English spoken very well
Region: Tuscany

Both Radda and Greve are excellent bases from which to explore scenic Chianti wine country with its regal castles and stone villages, in addition to Siena, Florence, and San Gimignano. Radda in particular offers a myriad of possibilities for accommodation, including private homes whose owners have coordinated a booking service: if space is not available at one, similar arrangements can be made elsewhere. The Val delle Corti is the home and vineyard estate of the ex-mayor of Radda, Giorgio Bianchi (who runs the booking service) and his lovely wife, Eli. The cozy pale-stone house with white shutters tops a hill overlooking town. The hosts, who moved here 20 years ago from Milan, are extremely active in community affairs and are a superb source for area information. They offer guests a quarter of their home: a comfortable two-bedroom apartment with a separate entrance, a large bathroom, kitchen with all necessities, and living room with fireplace, all furnished simply with family belongings. On request, Eli will supply coffee and jam for the weekly stay, while other meals can be taken at their nephew's newly opened restaurant in town, Le Vigne. *Directions:* Equidistant from Florence and Siena off the N222 Chianti road. Before entering Radda, turn right toward Lecchi-San Sano, then take the first left at Val delle Corti.

PODERE VAL DELLE CORTI
Hosts: Eli & Giorgio Bianchi
Localita: La Croce
Radda in Chianti (SI) 53017, Italy
Tel & fax: (0577) 738215
1 apartment
$600 (US) per week
Half board available at Le Vigne restaurant
Open Easter to October
English spoken very well
Region: Tuscany

On the opposite side of town from the Podere Val delle Corti (see preceding page), live Giorgio Bianchi's sister and family, who offer a two-bedroom apartment in a stone tower dating from 1832. This unique accommodation, perfect for a family of four, has an enchanting view of Radda and the countryside. The three-story tower has wood floors and beamed ceilings, a living room/kitchenette on the ground floor, one bedroom and a bath on the second floor, and a second bedroom on top. Furnishings are simple and in keeping with tower's rustic features. A small olive grove separates the tower from the Vitalis' lovely home, where a swimming pool awaits road-weary guests. Lele is a vivacious hostess who divides her time between guests; a small in-house weaving business; and helping out her son and daughter-in-law, a young and ambitious couple who converted a farmhouse into the most authentic regional restaurant in town—Le Vigne. A half-board meal plan can be arranged for guests of the tower. *Directions:* From either Siena or Florence, follow signs for Radda off the spectacular Strada del Chianti N222. Go through town until you reach the hotel/restaurant Villa Miranda (not recommended), after which turn right at the sign for Canvalle and follow the dirt road up to the tower.

TORRE CANVALLE
Hosts: General & Lele Bianchi Vitali
Localita: La Villa
Radda in Chianti (SI) 53017, Italy
Tel: (0577) 738321
1 apartment
$600 (US) weekly, $700 (US) (July & August)
Half board available at Le Vigne restaurant
Open Easter to November
English spoken very well
Region: Tuscany

The southeast corner of Tuscany offers a rich variety of sites to explore for those who seek the road less traveled, from the Amiata mountains for nature lovers, to the hilltowns of Montepulciano, Pienza, Montalcino for wine and art lovers, to Chianciano and Vignoni for thermal baths. La Palazzina, adoringly run by mother and daughter team, Bianca and Nicoletta, serves as the perfect base from which to visit these treasures. The restaurant is very special indeed. All the freshest, most natural ingredients from the farm are used in recipes originating from the Renaissance. The refined meals are served in two elegant dining rooms, accompanied by baroque music. The unusual checked tiled floors throughout the villa give it a cool, clean look and mix well with the many antique pieces. The 12 dainty bedrooms with immaculate bathrooms have women's names, each having its own color scheme. A swimming pool hugs the side of a hill overlooking the sweeping valley. Week-long courses are now offered in a variety of fields (Tuscan cooking, herbs and plants, astronomy). There are five lovely apartments for two to four persons in a nearby stone farmhouse for weekly stays. *Directions:* From Florence on the A1 autostrada, exit Chiusi and follow for Sarteano on route 478, turning left for Radicofani. After 14 kilometers turn left for Celle Sul Rigo then right at the sign for La Palazzino.

LA PALAZZINA
Hosts: Innocenti family
Localita: Le Vigne
Radicofani (SI) 53040, Italy
Tel: (0578) 55771 Fax: (0578) 53553
12 rooms with private bathrooms
* 3 apartments for 4 persons*
Lire 98,000 per person half board
All meals served
Open April to October
Credit cards: all major
Some English spoken
Region: Tuscany

The Amalfi coast has always been a favorite seaside escape for Italians and Americans, and Positano and Ravello are the cream of the resort areas. The best accommodations in Ravello are described in our *Italy: Charming Inns & Itineraries*: however, the Villa Amore, a small family-run hotel is a budget alternative in a high-rent area. It is ten minutes by foot from the main square in the direction of the romantic gardens of Villa Cimbrone. If you call from the main piazza, the hotel will send someone to collect your bags. A stone-walled path takes you to the simple hotel where a flight of stairs leads to the reception and homey sitting areas and the veranda restaurant surrounded by a flower garden. Here, high above the sea, guests are treated to one of the coast's more spectacular views. Several of the twelve rooms that hostess, Ermelinda, offers, open out to this same garden with its potted geraniums and lounge chairs. Rooms with baths are rather basic in decor, but are functional and clean. Local savory specialties, many of them seafood-based, are served either inside or out on the terrace looking down to the turquoise sea. *Directions:* From the square follow signs for Villa Cimbone, watching for Villa Amore, which is on the way.

VILLA AMORE
Hostess: Ermelinda Schiavo
Via del Fusco
Ravello (SA) 84010, Italy
Tel & fax: (089) 857135
12 rooms with private bathrooms
Lire 100,000 double B&B
82,000 per person half board
All meals served
Open all year
Credit cards: VS
Little English spoken
Region: Campania

The Villa Maria is perhaps best known for its absolutely delightful terrace restaurant which has a bird's-eye view of the magnificent coast. Whereas most of Ravello's hotels capture the southern view, the Villa Maria features the equally lovely vista to the north. The Villa Maria is two minutes by foot from the main square on the path winding to the Villa Cimbrone. After parking in the square (or at the Hotel Giordano), look for signs for the Villa Maria, perched on the cliffs to your right. The building is a romantic old villa with a garden stretching to the side where tables and chairs are set, a favorite place to dine while enjoying the superb view. Inside, there is a cozy dining room overlooking the garden. The bedrooms are furnished with antique pieces including brass beds. The bathrooms have been freshly remodeled and some even have Jacuzzi tubs. The hotel is owned by Vincenzo Palumbo whose staff speaks excellent English. Vincenzo also owns the nearby Hotel Giordano which has a heated pool that you can use. Guests at the Villa Maria have the best of all worlds: a wonderful view and location in a charming villa with a fine restaurant. *Directions*: Ravello is about 6 kilometers north of Amalfi on a small road heading north from the highway.

VILLA MARIA
Host: Vincenzo Palumbo
Via San Chiara 2
84010 Ravello (SA) 84010, Italy
Tel: (089) 857255 Fax: (089) 857071
15 rooms with private bathrooms
2 apartments
Lire 200,000–225,000 double B&B
* Lire 150,000–170,000 per person half board*
All meals served
Open all year
Credit cards: all major
English spoken very well
Region: Campania

The area of Tuscany south of Siena is a delightful discovery for those wanting to explore the lesser-known. Besides the charming hilltowns of Montepulciano, Pienza, and Montalcino, there are the abbeys of Monte Oliveto and Sant'Antimo, plus the thermal baths of Bagno Vignoni. The variety of landscapes within an 8-kilometer stretch of road makes it one of the most fascinating driving excursions in the region. And while touring this richly historical and natural area, a perfect base is the magnificent castle of the Aluffi Pentini family, theirs for the past 400 years or so. The family resides in the main villa while guests are accommodated in several separate houses along the internal road in a combination of apartments with one or two bedrooms, living room and kitchenette, plus six simply and characteristically-appointed bedrooms with country furniture. Rooms facing out have some of the most breathtaking views imaginable. Downstairs is the dining room with wood tables covered with cheery checked cloths, where breakfast and dinner are served using home-grown products. *Directions*: The castle is well marked at 5 kilometers from San Quirico d'Orcia. Ripa d'Orcia is actually marked on most maps.

CASTELLO DI RIPA D'ORCIA   **NEW**
Hosts: The Aluffi Pentini family
Localita: Ripa d'Orcia
Via della Contea 1
Castiglione d'Orcia (SI) 53023, Italy
Tel: (0577) 897376 Fax: (0577) 898038
6 rooms with private bathrooms
7 apartments for 2 to 4 persons
Lire 135,000 double B&B
* 140,000–250,000 daily for apartment*
2-day minimum stay (rooms)
Breakfast and dinner served
Open March to January 7
English spoken well
Region: Tuscany

Tuscany is the most visited region in Italy—mostly between Siena and Florence—but it nonetheless contains many other treasures off the beaten track. Heading west from Florence toward the coast are the lovely towns of Lucca and Pisa, and just north of them is the beautifully scenic area known as Garfagnana, which features two nature reserves and the Apuan Alps. Here in the northernmost tip of Tuscany is evidence of how Italian culture varies not only from one region to another, but within a region itself. In the heart of these mountains, the genial Coletti family runs a lively restaurant and cultivates cereals, wild berries, and chestnuts. Just recently, the Colettis have added a bed and breakfast to their list of activities. Seven double rooms with a mountain-cabin feeling, with pinewood floors and ceilings, have been fashioned in a restored three-story building in the stone village of Roggio. Most have a balcony and all have very nice modern bathrooms. Meals are taken around the corner at the family restaurant where Gemma Coletti prepares her special lasagna and polenta with porcini mushrooms, among other local specialties. *Directions*: From Lucca, take route 445 toward Castelnuovo and on to Roggio. Take a left up a winding road to Roggio, where a sign indicates the Da Gemma restaurant in the village.

AZIENDA COLETTI
Hosts: Gemma & Severino Coletti
Localita: Vagli Sotto
Roggio (LU) 55100, Italy
Tel: (0583) 649179
7 rooms with private bathrooms
Lire 70,000 double B&B
All meals served
Open all year, except Christmas
Very little English spoken
Region: Tuscany

A delightful alternative to our group of accommodations in Rome is Casa Stefazio, the only true in-home bed and breakfast. The location and setting are as perfect as the dedication and warm hospitality offered by Stefania and Orazio in their large, ivy-covered suburban home, just 30 minutes from the city center, surrounded by several acres of manicured garden. On the lower level, with a separate entrance, are three bedrooms and one spacious "suite" accommodating a family of four (this has a sauna), each with its own immaculate bathroom, TV, and mini bar, and each with its own color scheme. On the first floor near the hosts' quarters is an additional bedroom with its own bathroom. The main areas include living room, large American-style kitchen, where both Stefania and Orazio work wonders (he has a Cordon Bleu diploma), and eating area overlooking the expansive lawn and distant woods. Dinner is served on request under the pergola. Sports activities such as horseback riding, tennis and swimming are easily arranged. The hosts also organize excursions for groups of friends throughout Italy. *Directions*: Exit Settebagni from autostrada A1. Call one day ahead to receive detailed directions. With advance notice arrangements can be made to be picked up at the station or airport.

CASA STEFAZIO
Hosts: Stefania & Orazio Azzola
Via della Marcigliana 553
Rome 00138, Italy
Tel: (06) 87120042 Fax: (06) 87120012
2 rooms, 2 suites with private bathrooms
$160–200 (US) double B&B
Breakfast only
Dinner served upon request
Open March 15 to December
English spoken very well
Region: Lazio

The Due Torri is a perfect example of a small and charming city hotel, a breed not easy to find in today's urban centers. The building, dating from the early 1800s, is tucked away on a tiny, narrow street in the historical section of Rome between the Spanish Steps and Navona Square. Renovated several years ago, the 26 very small bedrooms are decorated with care and taste, featuring spotless bathrooms, period antiques, and peach-colored fabric walls matching bedspreads and draperies. Many amenities are offered, including elevator and air conditioning, which provides welcome relief on Roman hot summer days. The cozy and impressive reception and sitting area have Oriental carpets, cream-color draperies, gilt-framed mirrors and paintings, and elegant tapestry chairs. The fifth-floor mansard room 503 is especially appealing, as are the fourth-floor rooms with balconies. Breakfast is served off the reception area, a room made cheery with trellis- and ivy-covered paper. A courteous staff assists in making suggestions for local sightseeing and restaurants. Due Torri is a popular hotel, so be sure to reserve your room at least one month in advance. *Directions*: Use a detailed city map to locate the hotel, north of Navona square in a maze of winding streets.

HOTEL DUE TORRI
Hostess: Lidia Aperio Bella
Vicolo del Leonetto 23
Rome 00186, Italy
Tel: (06) 6876983/6875765
Fax: (06) 6865442
26 rooms with private bathrooms
Lire 250,000 double B&B
Breakfast only
Open all year
Credit cards: all major
English spoken well
Region: Lazio

Many hotels in Rome can boast panoramic views over the city, but few have such a close-up view of a world-famous monument as the Fontana Hotel. Located directly on the square containing the magnificent Trevi fountain, the Fontana's windows look out on to its gushing waters, where you can practically toss a coin from your room. The sleek black-and-white breakfast room with wrought-iron chairs and tables is situated on the top floor of the 14th-century building, giving a bird's-eye view over the square from an enormous picture window. The small rooms are sweetly done with pastel-floral wallpaper, bedspreads, and white curtains and vary in size and decor. Bathrooms were incorporated into each room later, and are quite small. Narrow, vaulted-ceilinged halls leading to the guestrooms are adorned with antique prints of Rome. A very gradual updating of rooms is in progress and the initial results are splendid. Signora Elena and her staff at the desk attend to guests' every need. The noise commonly associated with a city hotel is not a problem here as the square is closed to traffic, although loud voices of tourists lingering into the early hours can be a problem in the summer when the fountain closes at midnight. *Directions*: Use a detailed city map to locate the hotel in the Piazza di Trevi off the Via Tritone.

FONTANA HOTEL
Hostess: Elena Daneo
Piazza di Trevi 96
Rome 00187, Italy
Tel: (06) 6786113/6791056 Fax: (06) 6790024
27 rooms with private bathrooms
Lire 260,000 double B&B
Breakfast only
Open all year
Credit cards: all major
English spoken well
Region: Lazio

The Locarno Hotel is centrally located on the corner of a rather busy street, only two blocks from bustling Popolo Square. Its downtown location makes noise unavoidable, so it is advisable to request a room away from the street, even though the installation of thermal windows has helped. Even with the extensive renovations it has undergone, the hotel, dating from 1925, retains the art-deco flavor it had originally. The red-carpeted reception area leads to a cozy bar and long, mirrored sitting room lined with cushioned banquettes and café tables. There is also a side patio with shady canvas umbrellas where guests can take breakfast in warm weather, if not in the new and cheery breakfast room looking out to the patio. Another fabulous addition is the opening of the rooftop garden where you can gaze over Rome's tiled roofs and terraces to St. Peter's dome and Villa Borghese park. The 42 rooms with bathrooms are decorated with antiques, gold-framed mirrors, and pretty floral wallpaper. The Locarno features such extras as a parking garage and free use of bicycles with which you might tour the Villa Borghese park. It is no wonder that this has always been a favorite among artists and writers. Reserve well in advance. *Directions*: Use a detailed city map to locate the hotel one block east of the Tiber River at Flaminia square sign.

HOTEL LOCARNO
Hostess: Caterina Valente
Via della Penna 22
Rome 00186, Italy
Tel: (06) 3610841/2/3 Fax: (06) 3215249
42 rooms and 2 suites with private bathrooms
Lire 250,000 double B&B
Breakfast only
Open all year
Credit cards: all major
English spoken well
Region: Lazio

The Teatro di Pompeo, a well-managed, efficient, and friendly small hotel, gets its name from the ruins of the Pompeius Theater (55 B.C.) which were actually discovered under the building's foundation. The pale-yellow hotel is centrally located between Navona and Campo dei Fiori Squares, a popular area characterized by authentic local color and narrow streets lined with artisans' workshops, with many restored buildings painted in the wonderful, faded earth tones so typical of Rome. Signor Luigi at reception welcomes guests enthusiastically to the 12 new and spotless bedrooms, simply and tastefully decorated with antique prints of ancient Rome, and warmed overhead by original beamed ceilings. Many amenities, including air conditioning (supplemental charge), spotless bathrooms, TV, and telephone are available in each room. Descending a short flight of stairs from the mini-reception and bar area brings you to the dark, cave-like breakfast room, unique in that it is part of the ancient Pompeian theater. Next door is the Der Pallaro restaurant, a favorite with the local citizenry, where guests can treat themselves to a genuine Roman meal. *Directions*: Use a detailed city map to locate the hotel three blocks east of Campo dei Fiori square.

HOTEL TEATRO DI POMPEO
Host: Lorenzo Mignoni
Largo del Pallaro 8
Rome 00186, Italy
Tel: (06) 68300170 Fax: (06) 68805531
12 rooms with private bathrooms
Lire 240,000 double B&B
Breakfast only
Open all year
Credit cards: all major
English spoken well
Region: Lazio

A welcome addition to the group of family-run city hotels is the Venezia, efficiently run and owned by young and gracious Patrizia Diletti. Although hotels near train stations are generally less desirable, the area around Rome's Termini station has experienced dramatically positive changes, thanks to the city's new mayor—there is a high concentration of hotels and offices within the turn-of-the-century-style buildings. Although the Venezia has 61 rooms, it has the feeling of a small and friendly place from the moment one enters its doors. Patrizia inherited the hotel from her Swiss grandparents and has made it her priority to maintain their reputable tradition in hospitality. Her passion for collecting antiques such as Orientals rugs and rich period paintings is evident throughout the spacious sitting rooms. A buffet breakfast is served in a room with peach tablecloths and fresh flowers topping tables. Upstairs the spotless rooms are decorated uniformly in white and rose hues with Venetian glass chandeliers, and offer all modern amenities. Patrizia has purposely decorated predominantly with white (even bedspreads), so that any sign of dirt can be spotted immediately. The corner rooms are the most spacious and those on the top floor have small balconies lined with geranium pots. Centrally located, the hotel is a 15-minute walk to Rome's historical center. *Directions:* Consult a detailed city may to locate the hotel to the right of the station.

HOTEL VENEZIA **NEW**
Hostess: Patrizia Diletti
Via Varese 18
Rome 00185, Italy
Tel: (06) 4457101 Fax: (06) 4957687
61 rooms with private bathrooms
Lire 222,000 double B&B
Breakfast only
Open all year
Credit cards: MC, VS
English spoken well
Region: Lazio

Behind the city gates of Porta Pinciana, whose ancient walls lead from the Via Veneto, is tranquil, tree-lined Via Nomentana, once a luxurious residential street. Many elegant pastel-colored villas remain (including that of Mussolini), but most have been converted into embassy-owned apartments over the years. The Villa del Parco has been transformed into a lovely and quiet hotel with a bed-and-breakfast feel to it. A flower-edged driveway leads to the villa, passing by tables set up for breakfast in the small front garden. When you enter the pleasant lobby scattered with antiques and comfy sofas you feel that you've arrived home. Three cozy sitting rooms invite guests to sit and relax. All of the twenty-five guestrooms, each with private bath, have been renovated and vary greatly in size and decor, which tends to be a mixture of old and new furnishings. Request one of the larger rooms facing out the back of the hotel just in case the street noise might be disturbing. The Bernardini family and friendly staff are happy to make restaurant and itinerary suggestions and, as parking is always a problem, take note that a reputable garage (with limousine service) is located just across the street. *Directions*: Rely on a detailed city map to locate the hotel in a residential district, a 15-minute walk from the city center.

HOTEL VILLA DEL PARCO
Hosts: Bernardini family
Via Nomentana 110
Rome 00161, Italy
Tel: (06) 44237773 Fax: (06) 44237572
25 rooms with private bathrooms
Lire 225,000 double B&B
Breakfast only
Open all year
Credit cards: all major
Some English spoken
Region: Lazio

An alternative to staying in Rome's busy city center, especially for families, is the Santa Rufina farm on the very outskirts of Rome. For a capital city of its size, it is truly amazing to find this enormous oasis of green farmland emerging just at the cutoff point of urban developments. Sophisticated hosts Gianni and Giulia happily settled back in the inherited family farm after many years of working abroad and after recently renovating and converting the stalls and barn into four independent apartments, began their bed-and-breakfast business. Guests stay in various-sized lodgings with one or two bedrooms, nice new bathrooms, fully-equipped kitchenettes, and luminous living rooms, each with its own front garden. They are pleasantly furnished with the family's antiques, paintings, and drawings. Breakfast fixings are left at the beginning of guests' stay. Although the Remedias work in the city, Gianni's brothers still manage the farm and live just across the road within the property. A small pool will be available to guests by summer 1996 and reduced rates are given for weekly stays. *Directions*: Santa Rufina is located directly west of Rome, just outside the circular highway around the city (G.R.A.)—exit at Boccea to number 1115 (iron gate entrance). Thirty-five kilometers from Fiumicino airport, 20 kilometers from city center. A car is recommended to reach public transportation to the city.

TENUTA SANTA RUFINA   **NEW**
Hosts: Giovanni Remedia family
Via Boccea 1115
Rome 00167, Italy
Tel & fax: (06) 61909138 or Tel: (0335) 246977
4 apartments for 2 to 5 persons
Lire 170,000–240,000 daily per apartment
3-day minimum stay
No meals served
Open all year
English spoken very well
Region: Lazio

The spectacular 2,500-acre property of Montestigliano is a rich combination of woods, cultivated fields, olive groves, and open meadows all surrounding the hamlet dating to 1730. From its hilltop perch, splendid full valley and plain views are enjoyed. British-born hostess, Susan, makes sure guests are comfortably settled in one of the six independent apartments within the various houses. All retain their original Tuscan character in furnishings and have a combination of one to three bedrooms, kitchen, living room with fireplace, and essential modern amenities (full bathrooms, washing machines, firm mattresses). A special opportunity to reside in the main villa, once owned by nobility, is open to groups of up to 12 persons. Two swimming pools are at guests' disposal, plus many paths and trails for taking long countryside walks. Montestigliano is a marvelous base for those who wish to explore in depth a part of Tuscany whose traditions and lifestyles have remained intact. While still having Siena, San Gimignano, Pienza, Montalcino, and the Chianti area at one's fingertips, there's a chance to explore the many nearby medieval villages of this culturally rich territory. Plenty of shops and dining possibilities are available below in the towns of Rosia and Sovicille. *Directions*: From Siena (12 kilometers) take route 73 to Rosia, turning left at the sign for Orgia/Torri. The road up left to Montestigliano is the one right after Stigliano.

MONTESTIGLIANO   **NEW**
Hostess: Susan Pennington
Rosia (SI) 53010, Italy
Tel: (0577) 342013 Fax: (0577) 342100
6 apartments, 1 house
Lire 85,000–225,000 daily per apartment
4-day minimum stay, 1 week July and August
No meals served
Open all year
English spoken fluently
Region: Tuscany

Parma is without doubt the city most internationally known for its cheese and prosciutto, which you should not fail to sample while you're in the region. Thirty kilometers from Parma are found the curative thermal waters of Salsomaggiore and just beyond town is the Antica Torre, the ancient 13th-century tower which majestically crowns a hilltop overlooking the soft green countryside. The Pavesi family, proprietors of the surrounding farm, offer warm hospitality to its guests within the tower. One bedroom with bath is located on each of the tower's four floors and, in addition, the family has a large two-bedroom apartment available in the main house, ideal for a family. There are four additional apartments recently added within the stone residence. Rooms are simply decorated, and have lovely views over the valley. The barn has been converted into a pleasant dining room where fortunate guests sit down together to a hearty, homemade, Emiliana-style meal, including fresh pastas, vegetables, meat, and poultry direct from the farm. Amenities include a swimming pool, bicycles, and horses. *Directions:* From Salsomaggiore, go through town, following signs for Cangelasio and then Antica Torre, 3.5 kilometers from Salsomaggiore.

ANTICA TORRE
Hosts: Francesco Pavesi family
Localita: Cangelasio-Case Bussandri 197
Salsomaggiore Terme (PR) 43039, Italy
Tel & fax: (0524) 575425
4 rooms with private bathrooms
5 apartments
Lire 100,000 double B&B
 70,000 per person half board
2-day minimum stay, 1 week in July and August
All meals served
Open March to November
Very little English spoken
Region: Emilia-Romagna

Though near both Verona and Lake Garda, the Ca'Verde farm feels far away from civilization, immersed in a wooded valley in the Veneto wine country. Nine families got together 12 years ago to purchase the unusual stone Provence-style farmhouse, originally a 15th-century convent, and turned it into a busy dairy farm producing cheese and yogurt. They adhere to traditional production methods without additives or preservatives. Five attic rooms are available for guests in the enormous U-shaped house where three of the families live. Rooms for two to four people are small and utilitarian, with rustic wood beds, beamed ceilings with skylights, and one clean, modern bathroom for every two rooms. Four new more comfortable rooms with bathrooms have been added (at a slightly higher rate) to another wing. Meals, prepared by a professional chef using regional recipes and homemade wine, are served in three informal dining rooms with red-checked tablecloths and large fireplaces. Guests dine in or out on the patio, and in the summer are treated to outdoor concerts and cinema. *Directions:* From Verona take the A12 autostrada toward Brennero. Exit at Verona Nord, and follow signs for San Ambrogio. Go through town and start up the hill, watching for a small sign for Ca'Verde on the left side of the road. (Total of 15 kilometers.)

CA'VERDE (Co-op 8 Marzo)
Hostess: Vilma Zamboni
Azienda Agricola 8 Marzo
San Ambrogio Valpolicella (VR) 37010, Italy
Tel: (045) 6861760 Fax: (045) 6861245
Tel: (02) 66802366 Fax (02) 66802909 when closed
9 rooms, 4 with private bathrooms
Lire 115,000 per person half board
All meals served
Open May to October
Some English spoken
Region: Veneto

Agritourism and bed-and-breakfast-type accommodations are virtually non-existent in the northern lake district, so coming across the enchanting Villa Simplicitas was a special treat. The pale-yellow country house of Milanese family Castelli, sits high up in the hills between Lakes Como and Lugano and is surrounded by thick woods. There is a wonderful old-fashioned charm to the place, enhanced by many heirloom turn-of-the-century antiques scattered about the cozy living and dining rooms. Pretty floral fabrics cover sofas and armchairs, in perfect harmony with the soft yellow walls bordered with stenciled designs. The same warmth is spread among the ten guest bedrooms with their pinewood floors and *trompe l'oeil* paneled walls, antique beds, and lace doilies adorning dressers. Innovative meals are prepared by chef Mantelli using his worldwide experience, and are served either inside or out on the veranda with green and white striped awnings and matching director's chairs. In the evening, impeccably set tables are candlelit for a romantic dinner for two—simply heavenly. *Directions:* From Como head north to Argegno. Turn left, passing through S. Fedele, then just after town at the bus station, turn left—it is 2 kilometers up to the house.

VILLA SIMPLICITAS
Hosts: Curzio Castelli family
Localita: Simplicitas
San Fedele d'Intelvi (CO) 22028, Italy
Tel: (031) 831132
10 rooms with private bathrooms
Lire 140,000 double B&B
All meals served
Open: April to October
English spoken well
Region: Lombardy

Due to the ever-increasing popularity of the stunning medieval village of San Gimignano, accommodations in the surrounding countryside have flourished. La Casanova is a typical square stone farmhouse with wood shutters and red-tile roof, which you'll grow accustomed to seeing throughout Tuscany. The bed and breakfast's exceptional feature is that it enjoys a privileged view of the towers of San Gimignano, an ancient town referred to as the "Manhattan" of the year 1000. Marisa and Monica Cappellini are jovial hostesses who pride themselves on offering comfortable and immaculate accommodations to their international clientele. Breakfast is served on the outside patio where guests are immersed in breathtaking scenery, before heading out to visit intriguing San Gimignano and the many surrounding villages. This is an authentic and simple wine-producing farm with eight double rooms with private baths. Country furniture characteristic of the region decorates the rooms, whose original architectural features have been preserved. *Directions:* From San Gimignano take the road toward Volterra. After 2 kilometers, turn left at the sign for Casanova, **not** Hotel Pescille.

CASANOVA DI PESCILLE
Hostess: Marisa Cappellini
Localita: Pescille
San Gimignano (SI) 53037, Italy
Tel & fax: (0577) 941902
8 doubles with private bathrooms
Lire 100,000 double B&B
Breakfast only
Open all year
Credit cards: MC, VS
No English spoken (some French)
Region: Tuscany

Accidentally coming upon the Casolare, tucked away into the hills 8 kilometers beyond medieval San Gimignano, was a delightful surprise. Just before reaching the bed and breakfast, you'll see an abandoned stone convent dating back to 1100. Leaving the convent and the tourists behind, guests arriving at the Casolare feel as if they're coming "home." The attractive renovated farmhouse, hosted by Berta and Andrea, a young antique dealer, retains all of the features characteristic of the original structure. The five double rooms with bath are extremely comfortable and reflect superb taste. The two suites for two to four persons with terrace and living room have been decorated with refined antiques as well. Guests receive a folder of watercolor prints by a local artist depicting the various sites in the area with a description of each on the back. The original paintings adorn an entire wall in the living room. An extra bonus is the lovely pool which provides refreshment and relaxation after a hot day sightseeing, while anticipating another appetizing meal at dusk under the pergola. Berta is an excellent cook and prepares very special Tuscan menus. This is a truly tranquil spot. *Directions:* From San Gimignano follow signs for Montaione. Staying left at the fork, turn left onto a dirt road for Libbiano and take it to the end.

CASOLARE DI LIBBIANO
Hosts: Andrea & Berta Bucciarelli
Localita: Libbiano 3
San Gimignano (SI) 53037, Italy
Tel & fax: (0577) 946002
5 rooms and 2 suites with private bathrooms
Lire 115,000–125,000 per person half board
3-day minimum stay
Breakfast and dinner served
Open Easter to October
Some English spoken
Region: Tuscany

The increasing popularity of this perfectly intact medieval town and the resulting availability of accommodations has made San Gimignano a hub from which tourists fan out to visit nearby, less-well-known treasures such as Volterra, Colle Val d'Elsa, and Monteriggioni. A very pleasant stay is very likely at the Podere Villuzza, run by friendly young Sandra and Gianni Dei who opened the doors of their 150-year-old stone farmhouse to guests after careful restoration. Chairs are set up in front where visitors can enjoy the view of vineyard-covered hills leading up to the impressive multi-towered town. A hearty dinner may be shared with other guests in the simple country-style dining room where Sandra prepares tantalizing, fresh specialties from the family recipe book. Her husband occupies himself with the production of top-quality Vernaccia wine. Two double rooms with nice new bathrooms are upstairs, furnished with wrought-iron beds and antique armoires, complemented by mansard ceilings. The larger double has a private terrace overlooking the back hills. Also available are three small apartments within the house that include a living area and kitchen for weekly stays. *Directions:* Go through town and follow signs for Certaldo. After 2 kilometers turn right and follow signs for Villuzza.

PODERE VILLUZZA
Hosts: Sandra & Gianni Dei
Strada 25
San Gimignano (SI) 53037, Italy
Tel: (0577) 940585 Fax: (0577) 942247
4 rooms with private bathrooms, 3 apartments
Lire 90,000–112,000 double B&B
Breakfast and dinner served
Open all year
Some English spoken
Region: Tuscany

In the heart of the wine valley of Piedmont, between the principal cities of Piedmont: Alessandria, Alba, and Asti, you find lovely, serene countryside characterized by rolling green hills lined with vineyards and a strong tradition of fine country dining. Maria and Piercarlo are a local couple who have dedicated their lives to their farm and its production of Barolo and Dolcetto wines, as did their parents and grandparents. In fact, their typical white rectangular farmhouse has been in the family for well over 100 years. Over those years, as the family grew, so did the main house, eventually being connected to the barn and stables to make room for everyone. A family of just three, the Carellis found themselves with extra space and decided to use two of the bedrooms for guests, leaving grandmother's simple antiques in them, and adding one spotless bathroom in between. The dining room is popular with locals, and will serve up an unforgettable meal of homemade tagliatelle, lamb, and other regional specialties. Guests get a peek at a real farmer's lifestyle—some knowledge of Italian is recommended. Advance reservations are requested. *Directions:* From San Marzano, take the road leading north from town toward Agliano. Turn right at the chapel and follow signs for the farm.

ANTICA FATTORIA DEL COLLE
Hosts: Maria & Piercarlo Carelli
Reg. Chierina 17
San Marzano Oliveto (AT) 14050, Italy
Tel: (0141) 856252
2 rooms sharing 1 bathroom
Lire 85,000 per person full board only
All meals served
Open all year
No English spoken
Region: Piedmont

On the other side of town from the Antica Fattoria (see previous page) is another typical farmhouse and vineyard run cooperatively by several local families. There are simple and very neat guest bedrooms upstairs, decorated with country furniture typical of the area. One of the five bedrooms has an en-suite bathroom. The farm work seems to be evenly divided among these energetic families, whose members convene along with locals at lunch time in the spacious and rustic restaurant on the premises. Here they can count on a hearty multi-course meal prepared from the freshest possible ingredients directly off their land. This provides a convenient and very economical location from which to launch excursions to some of the delightful villages in the immediate vicinity, and of course, to Alba and Asti, which should not be missed. You can also take shorter trips on horseback from nearby stables into the scenic surrounding countryside. Or alternatively, you could visit the Italian Riviera, just an hour and a half away. Advance reservations are required. *Directions:* Coming from the direction of Nizza Monferrato, take the middle road at the triple fork just before San Marzano. La Viranda is just up the road on the left.

LA VIRANDA
Hostess: Lorella Solito
Localita: Corte 64
Piazza Martiri Liberta 2
San Marzano Oliveto (AT) 14042, Italy
Tel: (0141) 856571
5 rooms, 1 with private bathroom
Lire 56,000 double B&B
* 40,000 per person half board*
All meals served
Closed August & January
Some English spoken
Region: Piedmont

From the sheer monumental size of the Cavaglioni villa, erected from the original 14th-century fortress, one has an idea of just how important an agricultural center this farm property was in its heyday. The property was just one of many owned by the noble Galeotti-Ottieri family since the 18th century and today Signora Anna Maria opens up the third floor of the villa to guests, offering accommodation within six double and three single rooms, all down a long hall divided by a large living area. Rooms are simply appointed with wrought-iron beds and old family antiques. Wood beams divide fresco designs on some of the ceilings while worn terra-cotta bricks cover floors. A definite sensation that time has stood still pervades. New bathrooms, each with colored tiles coordinating with bedrooms, are either en suite, shared, or private but outside rooms. The nicest room is the one at the end, considered a suite for its size. A basic breakfast is served in a small room on this floor. To the back is a large garden where two separate apartments are available for longer stays. Gracious Signora Anna Maria adores assisting guests with local itineraries and suggestions. *Directions*: From Siena take route 223 towards Grosseto. After 10 kilometers turn right for San Rocco then after 1 kilometer, before town, turn left at the sign for Cavaglioni. Pass an iron gate to the side entrance.

FATTORIA DI CAVAGLIONI   **NEW**
Hostess: Anna Maria Galeotti-Ottieri
Via del Poggetto 1
San Rocco a Pilli (SI) 53010, Italy
Tel: (0577) 347723 Fax: (0577) 348364
9 rooms, 4 with private bathrooms
2 apartments
Lire 100,000 double B&B
Breakfast only
Open all year
English spoken well
Region: Tuscany

In the olive-strewn countryside around the magical town of Ostuni is the Tenuta Deserto farm, where the Roman Lancelloti family has summered for centuries. This *masseria* was built in several periods dating back to the 1600s, and is made up of the main house, a chapel, a 16th-century stone tower, and several houses which were once farmers' quarters. The main brick villa has been divided into sections—a large part reserved for a three-bedroom apartment with three bathrooms, fully equipped kitchen, and living room. Five more two- and three-bedroom apartments have been created in outlying white houses, one being of actual *trullo* construction, with cone-shaped stone roof, typical of the Alberobello area. Young and gracious Sveva and Riccardo have been hosting travelers for many years and are most attentive to their needs. The spacious rooms are decorated with taste and care, using family antiques, botanical prints, local handicrafts, and brightly colored floral bedspreads. Guests convene at poolside or in the lovely "clubhouse" living room with fireplace and vaulted ceilings. Meals can be arranged upon request. *Directions:* From Bari take the coastal route N379, exiting at San Vito. Cross through town, following signs for Ceglie. After 3.5 kilometers turn right on a dirt road at the bed-and-breakfast sign.

TENUTA DESERTO
Hosts: Sveva & Riccardo Lancellotti Delfino
San Vito dei Normanni (BR) 72019, Italy
Tel: (0831) 983062 Fax: (06) 3219566
6 apartments
Lire 400,000–1,200,000 weekly per apartment
  (2 to 7 people)
Weekly stay required in July & August
Dinner served upon request
Open April to October
English spoken very well
Region: Apulia

Right in the heart of the chic (and expensive) Italian Riviera is a small jewel of a bed and breakfast, hugging the hillside above the ports of Portofino and Santa Margherita. The young and handsome host, Roberto Gnocchi, has completely restored the small stone farmhouse on a piece of the family's property. Three tastefully decorated double rooms, each with private bath, are offered to guests, along with panoramic views over the fruit orchard and down to the sea. A cozy high-ceilinged living room, inviting one to curl up with a book or converse, gives visitors the feeling of being at the home of friends. The ambiance is intimate and welcoming. In the beamed dining room, breakfast and dinners (featuring local specialties) are served. To accommodate the increasing number of requests, four additional rooms have been created in the former private home next door, decorated in the same warm fashion with scattered antiques. From Genoa to the marvels of Cinque Terre, the Ligurian coast holds some very special treasures, and the Gnocchi makes a perfect and very reasonable place from which to discover them. *Directions:* From Santa Marghereta follow signs to Genova going uphill for about 4 kilometers until you see a blue sign indicating an intersection. Just after, on the left, there is a narrow road with a barrier.

GNOCCHI
Host: Roberto Gnocchi
Via Romana 53
Santa Margherita (GE) 16038, Italy
Tel: (0185) 283431/287923 or (0330) 486432
7 rooms with private bathrooms
Lire 110,000 double B&B
75,000 per person half board
Breakfast and dinner served
Open March to October
English spoken well
Region: Liguria

As more travelers realize just how short the distances are between destinations of interest throughout Italy, weekly house rentals have become more popular, giving visitors easy access to many places from one base that they can call "home." One such ideal base is La Sovana bordering Tuscany and Umbria and equidistant to Florence, Chianti, Siena, Cortona, Perugia, and Assisi, plus many other smaller hilltowns. Two stone farmhouses were restored to provide ten apartments for two to seven people. Tastefully decorated with local antique beds and armoires, matching floral bedspreads and curtains, they include a fully equipped kitchenette and eating area. Guests can dine upon request in the dining room in the main house, whose enormous arched window takes in the view of the vast open landscape. Giovannella and Giuseppe Olivi and their two children are present on weekends and throughout the summer and make their guests feel right at home. Otherwise, guests are in the capable hands of the caretakers. Potted flowers abound around the farmhouse and poolside, where on Saturday nights a barbecue is organized. Tennis courts are available. The most recent addition is four apartments in a converted barn. *Directions:* Just 2 kilometers from the Chiusi exit of the A1 autostrada. La Sovana is just before Sarteano on the right.

LA SOVANA
Hosts: Giuseppe Olivi family
Localita: Sovana
Sarteano (SI) 53047, Italy
Tel: (0578) 274086 Fax: (075) 600197
14 apartments
Lire 600,000–2,300,000 weekly
Dinner served upon request
Open Easter to November
Very little English spoken
Region: Tuscany

Saturnia's thermal waters have been gushing from an underground volcano for over 2,000 years, yet only recently have it and the enchanting surrounding *maremma* area become internationally famous, leading to new accommodations springing up. One such is the charming Villa Clodia, once home to nobility, now run by former restaurateur Giancarlo Ghezzi. The villa is a curiosity, seemingly built out of the limestone rock, one side overlooking the street and the other an expansive valley of grapevines and olive trees. Because of its unusual proportions, each room is unique in size and decor. A small winding stairway takes guests up or down to rooms, some of which have been literally carved out of the rock. All bedrooms feature scattered antiques, new bathrooms, and valley views, and a fortunate few boast a terrace. Breakfast is offered in a sweet, luminous room next to the sitting room. A lush rose garden and fruit orchard surround the inviting star-shaped pool. Advance reservations are a must and weekly stays are preferred. *Directions:* From Rome take the Aurelia highway north, turning off to the right at Vulci where you follow signs for Manciano, Montemerano, and Saturnia. Villa Clodia is in the middle of town.

VILLA CLODIA
Host: Giancarlo Ghezzi
Via Italia 43
Saturnia (GR) 58050, Italy
Tel: (0564) 601212 Fax: (0564) 601305
10 rooms with private bathrooms
Lire 115,000 double B&B
3-day minimum stay
Breakfast only
Closed February
Credit cards: VS
English spoken well
Region: Tuscany

The Podere Novelleto sits on the summit of the residential suburb of Sesto Fiorentino, above the spellbinding city of Florence, known for its concentration of Medici villas. The stone farmhouse is the last residence on the street to maintain a substantial amount of land under cultivation. Twenty-five hectares of olive groves parade down the hill behind the house, and, out front, visitors are treated to a fabulous panorama of red-roofed Florence. Meals are served on an open terrace, strategically oriented to capitalize on the unique view which becomes even more magical at night. Here, amidst a grape arbor and potted geraniums, guests may enjoy a delightful Florentine meal. Host Arrigo Luppi provides hospitality in a wing attached to the main house, all of which has been dedicated to that purpose. Five bedrooms with private bath are simply decorated with family antiques, although some are too modern in decor. Only 8 kilometers north of Florence, this bed and breakfast is an ideal base for exploring the region. *Directions:* It is tricky to find Podere Novelleto and best to call from Sesto Fiorentino to be accompanied.

PODERE NOVELLETO
Host: Arrigo Luppi
Via Carmignanello 4—Quinto Alto
Sesto Fiorentino (FI) 50019, Italy
Tel: (055) 454056
5 rooms with private bathrooms
Lire 120,000 double B&B
100,000 per person half board
Breakfast and dinner served
Open all year
Credit cards: VS
Some English spoken
Region: Tuscany

In centuries past, the property of the noble Pennisi family extended over a vast territory of the coast south of Taormina. What remains today are 12 acres of primarily citrus groves with a 17th-century hamlet in the center. Even though the Signori Pennisi reside in nearby Fiumefreddo, they are present on the farm during the day to attend to their guests. The pale-yellow, ivy-covered, one-story "Villa Ada" has been divided into two comfortable apartments, including two bedrooms, two bathrooms, and a large double living room with fireplace which opens up to a delightful terrace overlooking the groves and encompassing views of the Etna volcano and the sea, marred only by the highway several kilometers away. Pretty floral curtains, wrought-iron beds, and family antiques impart a true country flavor to the setting. Directly across the brick walk is a complex which houses the other two apartments, former barn/present dining room, enormous wine cellar, and even the family chapel. Rooms, here again, are authentically decorated with period pieces and harmonize well with the exposed beam ceilings and terra-cotta brick floors. With advance notice, meals are served at long tables in the cantina or out under the pergola on hot summer evenings. *Directions*: From Taormina on local route 114, pass Fiumefreddo and take the first right where Borgo is well marked.

BORGO VALERIO   **NEW**
Hosts: Piero Pennisi family
Via Civi 2
Fiumefreddo (CT) 95013, Sicily, Italy
Tel: (095) 641234 Fax: (095) 969872
4 apartments
Lire 60,000–80,000 per person
Occasional meals served
Open all year
Very little English spoken
Region: Sicily

Tenuta Gangivecchio is far off the beaten path, but well worth a detour. Not only will you discover a jewel of a small inn, but the adventure of finding Gangivecchio leads you through Sicily's beautiful Madonie region. The Tornabene family began by converting a room in their home (a 13th-century Benedettino monastery) into a restaurant serving a set-menu lunch based upon fresh produce from the farm. Although a two-hour-drive, the excellence of the simple, yet delicious meals soon brought guests from as far away as Palermo. The enterprising Tornabene family have now renovated the stables of the monastery into nine tastefully decorated guestrooms—appealing in their simplicity with rustic, red-tile floors, fresh whitewashed walls, hand-loomed scatter rugs, dark wood accents, rough-hewn beamed ceilings, attractively framed old prints on the walls, and pretty cotton floral bedspreads. Delicious, home-cooked meals are served to guests in a pretty dining room on the ground floor of the inn. Plan to arrive on a weekend for a lunch prepared by Signora Wanda and her daughter Giovanna, served in the dining room of the monastery. *Directions:* Drive east through Gangi on SS120. Just outside town, turn right at a small signpost for Gangivecchio. Go for about a kilometer and turn left at a tiny yellow sign. Continue up the hill for about 5 kilometers. Tenuta Gangivecchio is on your right.

TENUTA GANGIVECCHIO   **NEW**
Hosts: Betty and Paolo Tornabene
C. da Gangivecchio
90024 Gangi, (PA), Sicily, Italy
Tel: (0921) 89191
9 rooms
Lire 90,000 per person half board
All meals served
Closed 1 or 2 weeks end of June
Some English spoken
Region: Sicily

On the southwestern coast between the archaeological ruins of Selinunte and Sciacca with its hot springs, lies the anonymous town of Menfi. Menfi was virtually destroyed in the earthquake of 1971, and consequently is a mix of new construction and devastated areas still awaiting government funds. In the very center of all this sits the splendid 18th-century palazzo of the noble Ravida family, which miraculously survived disaster. One enters the front iron gates from the city street to discover a large stone courtyard with palm trees leading to the U-shaped villa with its solid Doric stone columns. The baron and his wife, who are in residence seasonally as they live in Rome, offer hospitality to guests in lovely rooms within the villa and garden house wing. The bedrooms are in perfect harmony with the general feeling of the home. There is a perfume of the past as you wander through the frescoed sitting rooms filled with period antiques and paintings left by ancestors. Fortunately for guests, the gracious hosts are experts in local itineraries. Their large agricultural property at a short distance from town comprises vast citrus and olive groves and, with hundreds of years of tradition in producing oil, it is no wonder that Ravida has received national and European recognition. *Directions:* Follow signs to the center of Menfi and ask for Via Roma or Palazzo Ravida.

RAVIDA   **NEW**
Hosts: Nicola & Ninni Ravida
Via Roma 173
Menfi (AG) 92013, Italy
Tel: (06) 3052537
6 rooms, 4 with private bathrooms
Lire 200,000 double B&B
Breakfast and occasional dinner served
3-day minimum stay
Open all year
English spoken well
Region: Sicily

The Alcala farm, made up of citrus and olive groves, vineyards, wheat crops, and a wide variety of fruit trees, extends over 75 acres of fertile plain backdropped by the Etna volcano—a picture-perfect setting. Cordial hostess Anna Sapuppo and her young family have taken over the family's agricultural business (her husband is a university professor) and have added the hospitality activity as well. The main house is a turn-of-the-century *masseria*, built in several sections, while guests are situated nearby in three different apartment setups, housing from two to six guests. Two of them are separate houses and have large open terraces. They include living room areas and kitchenettes and are pleasantly decorated with floral sofas and a mix of modern and old family furniture. Although breakfast is not served, guests can help themselves to plenty of fruits. An occasional dinner is served in the fascinating rustic wine cantina with its enormous wood barrels. Anna, a native Sicilian, gladly assists her guests with touring suggestions which include Catania city (important where **not** to go), the Taormina coast, Siracusa, Etna National Park, and the temples of Agrigento. A superb base at an unbeatable rate. *Directions*: Take autostrada A19 from Catania and exit at the first exit for Motta. Backtrack on the parallel road, passing the U.S. army base and turn left at the sign for Alcala.

ALCALA   **NEW**
Hosts: Anna Sappupo family
Casella Postale 100
Misterbianco (CT) 95045, Sicily, Italy
Tel & fax: (095) 7130029
3 apartments
Lire 40,000 per person
3-day minimum, 1 week July & August
No meals served
Open all year
Some English spoken
Region: Sicily

The little-visited coastal stretch from Messina to Cefalu has special appeal to the off-the-beaten-track traveler who will find the perfect place to stay at Casa Migliaca, a 200-year-old farmhouse nestling in the wooded hills 7 kilometers off the main road. This stone house just outside town, owned by Maria Teresa and Sebastiano, who left the city several years ago in favor of a rural lifestyle, offers a lovely sweeping view over olive and citrus groves down to the sea. The very congenial hosts love to converse with gusts around the kitchen table or down in the cool dining room (originally oil press) around the press wheel. A special effort was made to keep everything possible intact—all floors, ceilings, beams, kitchen tiles, and furniture are part of the original house, and although private bathrooms could not be incorporated, the house has its own distinct charm. There are even extra showers out in the garden! Guests are offered a choice of three double bedrooms upstairs, two downstairs, plus one apartment for 4 persons, with kitchen and living room. For those who are desire direct contact with Sicilian culture, Casa Migliaca is a truly memorable experience. *Directions*: From coastal route 113, 25 kilometers after Cefalu, turn right at the sign for Pettineo and follow it right past town. Just after a gas station, turn right on a descending gravel road to the house (unmarked).

CASA MIGLIACA   **NEW**
Hostess: Maria Teresa Allegra
Contrada Migliaca
Pettineo (ME) 98070, Sicily, Italy
Tel & fax: (0921) 336722
6 rooms sharing 3 bathrooms, 1 apartment
Lire 75,000 per person half board
3-day minimum stay
Breakfast and dinner served
Open all year
English spoken well
Region: Sicily

The San Vito Lo Capo point at the northwest corner of Sicily, bordered by two gulfs, boasts some of the most spectacular coastline on the island, including the 5,000-acre Natural Reserve Park (Lo Zingaro). Its rugged beauty, turquoise seas, and variety of animal and plant life make it a paradise for nature lovers. The stone village of Scopello lies above the sea at the entrance to the park and is a scenic and peaceful base from which to explore the western half of Sicily. Accommodations are scarce so I was pleased to meet Mimmo Scibiglia who has just converted a barn on the family's olive grove into a bed and breakfast. The very simple white rectangular house has a spiral staircase leading up to one of the six identical mini "suites" which include a bedroom, new bathroom, and living area with extra bed and kitchenette. All have two entrances, and on one side a small terrace looking out to the distant sea. Accommodations are budget-basic, decor spartan, and ambiance informal, but gregarious Mimmo makes guests feel like kings as he guides them carefully through the fascinating complexities of his native land. A do-it-yourself breakfast is served outside on the covered porch. A typical farm down the road serves marvelous local fare for dinners. *Directions*: From Palermo, exit from the autostrada at Castellammare and follow signs for Scopello/Zingaro. Turn left at the sign for Casale before town.

CASALE DEGLI OLIVI   **NEW**
Host: Mimmo Scibiglia
Via di Rocca Rossa 80
Scopello (TP) 91014, Sicily, Italy
Tel. (0924) 541386 or (0330) 740622
6 apartments
3-day minimum stay, 1 week July & August
Lire 60,000 double B&B
Breakfast only
Open April 15 to September
Some English spoken
Region: Sicily

For those who prefer the service of a small pensione, the Tranchina family awaits you with open arms. The pale-yellow three-story house sits in the quaint town of Scopello with its piazza and three streets. From ancient times this was an important fishing center especially for tuna, and the *Tonnara* stone fishing station down by the sea still stands as proof. Native Salvatore and his amiable Panamanian wife MariSin have been welcoming guests into their home for the past ten years. The entrance hall is a combination breakfast and dining room with a sitting area in the corner around the fireplace. A central staircase leads up to guestrooms, a few with balconies facing out to the distant sea. The rooms are simply appointed with light-wood armoires, wrought-iron beds, and crocheted white bedspreads. In the evening after a day at the seaside or touring, you come "home" to a delicious home-cooked meal of fresh fish or meat and vegetables from their garden. Enthusiastic MariSin spends time chatting with her guests and advising them what to visit in this culturally rich area. "Must-sees" include the ancient town of Erice, the ruins of Segesta, Selinunte, and Agrigento. *Directions*: From Palermo, exit from autostrada A29 at Castellammare and follow signs for Scopello. The pensione is found just after the bar with outdoor tables.

PENSIONE TRANCHINA   **NEW**
Hosts: MariSin & Salvatore Tranchina
Via A. Diaz 7
Scopello (TP) 91014, Sicily, Italy
Tel: (0924) 541099
10 rooms with private bathrooms
Lire 75,000 double B&B
  70,000 per person half board (high season)
Breakfast and dinner served
Open all year
English spoken fluently
Region: Sicily

The Limoneto was recommended to us by a reader who was "winging it" through the Sicilian countryside (not advisable). He raved about the "open arms" hospitality, the excellent meals, comfortable accommodations, and proximity to fascinating Siracusa. We have to agree. At just 10 kilometers from the historical center of Siracusa with its Greek and Roman influences, the orange-grove farm is a perfectly delightful, safe, and economical base from which to explore Sicily's southeastern corner. Adelina, Alceste, and their son, Francesco, make sure of this simply by making guests part of their family. Guestrooms are split between the refurbished barn and part of the main house, all with individual entrances. Rooms, some accommodating up to four persons, are new with pleasant modern decor and all have spotless bathrooms. Dinner is served either in the spacious dining room where locals come for a Sunday meal, or out in the back garden. Adelina welcomes the curious into her kitchen to observe and participate in the making of typical regional meals. The warmth exudes and when the evening is just right, she might even read some poetry. *Directions*: From Catania, take the autostrada to Siracusa sud exit. Turn right, then immediately left for Canicattini. At the end of the road, turn right on route 14 for Palazzolo and, after half a kilometer, turn left for Limoneto.

LIMONETO   **NEW**
Hosts: Alceste & Adelina Norcia
Viale Teracati 142
Siracusa (SC) 96100, Italy
Tel: (0931) 717352
6 rooms with private bathrooms
Lire 70,000 double B&B
 65,000 per person half board
All meals served
Open all year
Some English spoken
Region: Sicily

Taormina is on what could be referred to as the Amalfi coast of Sicily and, although the town is lovely and rich with history, it is very touristy. This of course means that rates are on the high side, but, happily, the Villa Schuler makes it affordable and its location is superb. The villa was converted from a private residence to a hotel by the Schuler family at the turn of the century and now grandson Gerardo has taken over the reins. The pink façade faces out to the street and has a large raised terrace with potted flowers, palms, and cypresses. Breakfast is served either here or in the gazebo where you can enjoy views encompassing the coastline and the peak of the Etna volcano. To the back is an enchanting garden—the town's largest besides the nearby public botanical gardens—filled with a profusion of jasmine, bougainvillea, and geraniums with several places to sit in the shade. You can exit from the garden directly onto the main street of town and it is just a short walk to the cable car which takes you down to the beach. Rooms have been updated over the past years, almost all with new bathrooms, and are spacious and simply but pleasantly decorated. Most have some sort of small balcony or terrace with sea views. The rooftop terrace offers yet another head-spinning view. *Directions*: Follow signs through town to the hotel.

VILLA SCHULER   **NEW**
Hosts: Gerardo Schuler family
Via Roma 2
Taormina (ME) 98039, Sicily, Italy
Tel: (0942) 23481 Fax: (0942) 23522
35 rooms with private bathrooms
Lire 115,000 double B&B
Breakfast only
Open all year
English spoken well
Region: Sicily

There is a beautiful stretch of coastline on the Adriatic Sea just south of Ancona, dramatically different from the more flat and uninteresting shoreline to the north and south with its modern hotels and condos. The quaint stone village of Sirolo sits high above the water on a mountainside looking down to the beaches of the Riviera Conero. Delightful seafood restaurants dot the shore, where you might enjoy a plate of pasta with fresh clams while watching the tide come in. Isabella and Giorgio Fabiani decided several years ago to open a bed and breakfast in 14th-century Sirolo, and offer five guestrooms above their small restaurant with its outdoor tables. The bedrooms are simply furnished in old-fashioned style, and most have sea views. The young couple is full of ideas to improve the premises, but since this is a historical building (legend has it that St. Francis stayed overnight here), even simple renovations are often restricted. No extra bathrooms are allowed—not even the faded green shutters adorning the windows can be touched. Nonetheless, the place exudes a basic charm. True Marchigiano-style meals feature seafood dishes (*brodetto)* for which the natives of the Marches are renowned. *Directions:* The Rocco is located in the town of Sirolo, after Portonovo.

LOCANDA ROCCO
Hostess: Isabella Fabiani
Via Torrione 1
Sirolo (AN) 60020, Italy
Tel: (071) 9330558/7823256
5 rooms sharing 2 bathrooms
Lire 80,000–90,000 double B&B
  70,000 per person half board
All meals served
Open April to October
Credit cards: AX, VS
Some English spoken
Region: Marches

The stone tower of Bagnara, dating back nearly a thousand years, is situated in the Upper Tiber Valley just 20 kilometers north of Perugia, and not far from the major cultural centers of Umbria, Assisi, Gubbio, and Citta del Castello. The independent tower is part of the vast tobacco farm of the Tremi family who reside in a luxurious villa just down the hill. Three fully equipped apartment-suites accommodating two to six people have been fashioned within the tower (available for weekly rental only). The quarters come complete with kitchenette and are nicely furnished in a refined country style with antiques, painted wrought-iron beds, and matching floral curtains and bedspreads. Original architectural features such as beamed ceilings, terra-cotta floors, and arched stone doorways lend authentic medieval ambiance to a stay here. And given the sweeping views it commands over the valley, it's easy to understand why this spot was chosen for a watchtower. The backdrop consists of wooded hills dotted with grazing livestock and distant farmhouses. An excellent and unusual base for thorough exploration of the natural and man-made wonders of this rich region. *Directions:* From Perugia, exit at Ponte Pattoli from highway 45. Follow signs for Umbertide, turning left at the second road, not right for Solfagnano. The Tremi villa is the first on the left.

LA TORRE DI BAGNARA
Hosts: Tremi family
Solfagnano (PG) 06080, Italy
Tel: (075) 604136
3 apartments
Lire 700,000–1,300,000 weekly
No meals served
Open March to October
English spoken well
Region: Umbria

The town of Spoleto has gained international fame thanks to the July *Due Mondi* festival, a month-long series of cultural events including ballet, theater, opera, and concerts with renowned artists which attracts a worldwide audience. Accommodations are reserved from one year to the next. For the rest of the year, however, Spoleto holds its own along with nearby Assisi, Spello, Todi, and Perugia as an enchanting medieval stone town, rich in historical past. The Vaita de Domo serves as an excellent bas from which to explore in depth the entire region of Umbria. Paolo Tamburi, from Rome, bought and restored the 17th-century palazzo, situated within the old walls of the town, seven years ago and created eight spacious apartments for weekly stays. The apartments vary in size and layout, accommodating from two to seven people. All take in views over the tiled rooftops and contain one to three bedrooms, fully equipped kitchen, living area, and one or two bathrooms. The largest, number 4, is spread out on three levels. Rooms are very comfortable, with beds, tables, and armoires made by a local carpenter. Cordial hostess, Daniela, of Spoleto, is on hand to assist guests, including furnishing breakfast supplies upon request. *Directions*: From autostrada A1, exit at Orte and follow route 418 to Spoleto. Best to call from town for directions.

RESIDENZA VAITA DE DOMO
Hostess: Daniela Tulli
Via Vaita de Domo 5
Spoleto (PG) 06049, Italy
Tel & fax: (06) 3052537
8 apartments
Lire 900,000–1,600,000 weekly
No meals served
Open all year
Some English spoken
Region: Umbria

Halfway between Florence and Siena in the heart of the Chianti region is the Sovigliano farm, recently restored by a handsome couple from Verona, Claudio Bicego and his wife, Patrizia, who delight in welcoming international visitors into their warm home. Guests have an independent entrance to the five bedrooms (only two with private bath), each very much in keeping with the pure simplicity of this typical farmhouse. Exposed-beam ceilings and terra-cotta floors, antique beds and armoires, and bucolic views make time stand still here. There is also a one-bedroom and a two-bedroom apartment within the house, decorated in similar style, with kitchen and dining area. The upstairs living room, sparsely furnished with the family's elegant antiques, kitchen with country fireplace, and surrounding garden are for everyone's use. Signor Bicego is actively involved in the production of top Tuscan wines in conjunction with several other wine estates, and also coordinates with other area residents to organize lessons in language, history, and culinary arts with local professors. *Directions:* From Siena, exit the superstrada at Poggibonsi; from Florence at Tavarnelle. Follow signs for Tavarnelle and, go through town towards Barberino, turning off at the sign for Sovigliano.

PODERE SOVIGLIANO
Hosts: Bicego family
Via Magliano 9
Tavarnelle Val di Pesa (FI) 50028, Italy
Tel & fax: (055) 8076217
5 rooms, 2 with private bathrooms
2 apartments (2-day minimum stay)
Lire 115,000 double B&B
* 125,000 apartment B&B*
Dinner upon request
Open all year
Credit cards: AX
English spoken well
Region: Tuscany

With their hearts set on running a bed and breakfast in the Liguria region, young Milanese couple Lucia and Nereo searched hard and long before finding Giandriale. Set high up in the remote mountains above the coast, the 18th-century stone farmhouse is surrounded by acres of low-range mountains covered with thick woods as far as the eye can see. Utter silence prevails. Just three bedrooms are reserved for guests within their home, simply decorated with country-style wood furniture. The one with en-suite bathroom is on the first floor, while the other two share a bathroom on the second floor next to the hosts' quarters. Meals are enjoyed in the downstairs dining room displaying an old-fashioned country stove that is used occasionally in the colder months for making polenta. Lucia prepares coffee cakes and jams for breakfast and uses mostly regional recipes in her cooking. Classic sightseeing destinations in the area include the riviera (Portofino, Santa Margherita, Chiaveri), or the Cinque Terre, 45 minutes away in the opposite direction. Nereo can also suggest several interesting off-the-beaten-track itineraries beyond Giandriale. Hiking trails and mountain bikes are available. *Directions*: From autostrada A14, exit at Sestri Levante and follow signs for Casarza Ligure, Castiglione, then, after 2 kilometers and many curves, Missano. Before the church in town, turn left at the sign for Giandriale. The house is 6 kilometers up the road (15 minutes).

GIANDRIALE   **NEW**
Hosts: Lucia Marelli & Nereo Giani
Localita: Giandriale
Tavarone di Maissana (SP) 19010, Italy
Tel & fax: (0187) 840279
3 rooms, 1 with private bathroom
Lire 50,000 double B&B
* 50,000 per person half board*
All meals served
Open all year
Some English spoken
Region: Liguria

Another one of Italy's best-kept secrets is the *Cinque Terre* coastline of southern Liguria bordering Tuscany, though this beautiful and quite unique area is now gaining increasing attention. Its five quaint stone villages hugging the hillside sweeping down to the sea were, until recently, accessible only by boat or by foot and are a delight to explore. Just south of the area right on the Poet's Gulf is the adorable seaside town of Tellaro, where visitors make a point of stopping to have a memorable meal at the Miranda restaurant. Husband and wife team, Giovanna and Angelo, have their own inimitable and ever-varying style of cooking based on fresh seafood which is present in the inexhaustible series of antipasti plates. Angelo has received plenty of press and praise (Michelin star) for these extraordinary dishes. Meals are served either on the porch with its green and white awnings, or in one of the three peach-colored dining rooms, simply and pleasantly appointed with scattered antiques. In the same vein are the six bedrooms, most with gulf view, which Aunt Miranda used to rent out and are now in the capable hands of son, Alessandro. A perfect base from which to enjoy this lesser-known area. *Directions:* Exit from the A12 autostrada at Sarzana, following signs for Lerici on route 331. Tellaro is 4.5 kilometers down the coast and the Miranda is on the main road before town.

LOCANDA MIRANDA
Hosts: Angelo & Giovanna Cabani
Via Fiascherino 92
Tellaro (SP) 19030, Italy
Tel: (0187) 968130/964012 Fax: (0187) 964032
6 rooms with private bathrooms
Lire 140,000 per person half board
3-day minimum stay
All meals served
Credit cards: MC, VS
Closed February
English spoken well
Region: Liguria

The Residenza San Andrea al Farinaio is located so far off the beaten path that you must write or call ahead for detailed instructions if you ever hope to find it, but its location makes it quite convenient as a home base for exploring both Tuscany and Umbria. And for those looking for well-priced accommodation without sacrificing comfort, this bed and breakfast might be a perfect choice. The oldest part of the inn dates back to the 13th century when it was home to the priests tending a church across the road. The present owner, Patrizia Nappi, is a warm and gracious hostess, speaks excellent English, and has lovingly transformed the old stone house into a cozy inn, combining modern pictures, furniture, and knickknacks with lovely antiques. Of the five bedrooms, three have private baths. A personal favorite is the large guestroom at the top of the stairs. The most wonderful area in the house is the dining room with its massive darkened-wood beams, large open fireplace, beautiful antique trestle table, colorful plates adorning the walls, and lots of copper pots and pans. If you make arrangements in advance, you can dine here with other guests, sharing a simple, superb meal family-style at the long, handsome candlelit table in front of a crackling fire. *Directions:* Head southeast from Cortona to Terontola (approximately 10 kilometers) and follow signs for Stadio. Continue until you see a sign on right for San Andrea.

RESIDENZA SAN ANDREA AL FARINAIO
Hostess: Patrizia Nappi
San Andrea al Farinaio, 118
Terontola di Cortona, (AR) 52044, Italy
Tel & fax: (0575) 677736
5 rooms, 3 with private bathrooms
Lire 150,000 double B&B
Breakfast and dinner served
Open all year
Fluent English spoken
Region: Tuscany

Practically 70 percent of the families residing in the Alto Adige mountain region offer bed-and-breakfast accommodations so, unless it's Christmas or August, a bed is not hard to come by. This is a region with a distinct Austrian flavor where more German than Italian is spoken, and where more *wurstel* than pasta is likely to be served at the table. The warm Trompedeller family heartily welcome international travelers to their typical Tyrolean-style home. The six guestrooms each have a private bath and are modestly decorated with basic light-wood furniture and accented with orange and brown curtains and bedspreads—a decor common to the bed and breakfasts in this region. The cozy wood-paneled dining room boasts a splendid panoramic view over the mountain cliffs and green foothills. The house is located several kilometers outside the quaint town of Tiers on a road which comes to an end at a babbling brook surrounded by hushed woods with hiking trails. Depending on the season, guests can take advantage of the Val Gardena ski slopes or summer mountain climbing. *Directions:* From the Verona-Brennero autostrada, exit at Bolzano Nord and follow signs for Tiers. Go through the town and make a hairpin left turn at the chapel.

VERALTENHOF
Hosts: Josef Trompedeller family
Oberstrasse 61
Tiers (BZ) 39050, Italy
Tel: (0471) 642102
6 rooms with private bathrooms
Lire 45,000 per person half board
Breakfast and dinner served
Open all year
No English spoken
Region: Trentino-Alto Adige

Since 1830, the 12th-century castle and 4,000-acre farm of Titignano have belonged to the noble Corsini family who eight years ago decided to offer guests six rooms in the main house, later adding a swimming pool and three new apartments in what was originally the farmer's quarters. They are pleasantly decorated with scattered country antiques. Management is in the hands of the Fontanis, a delightful young couple who take care of everything from looking after guests and the farm to cooking and serving. Meals are shared at a long table in one of the castle's graciously neglected rooms with an enormous gray stone fireplace sporting the family coat of arms, and lofty ceilings made of the stamped terra-cotta blocks typical of Umbria. Off the dining hall are the spacious bedrooms, each with modernized pink travertine bathrooms and decorated eclectically with unrefined antiques and wrought-iron beds. They have a worn charm about them. Common areas include a living room with bright floral sofas around a fireplace, a game and TV room for children, and a large terrace with a breathtaking, sweeping view covering three regions. *Directions:* From the Roma-Firenze A1 autostrada, exit at Orvieto. Follow signs for Arezzo, turning on route 79 for Prodo. Follow the long winding road for 35 kilometers past Prodo to Titignano.

FATTORIA TITIGNANO
Hosts: Monica & Giulio Fontani
Localita: Titignano
Orvieto (TR) 05010, Italy
Tel & fax: (0763) 308322
6 rooms with private bathrooms, 3 apartments
Lire 120,000 double B&B
* 85,000 per person half board*
Breakfast and dinner served
Open all year
Some English spoken
Region: Umbria

The Adriano is a small, family-run hotel with a long-standing tradition in hospitality and exceptionally good local cuisine. The operation has just recently been handed down to the third generation of the Cinelli family; siblings Umberto, Patrizia and Gabriella. Gabriella works her magic in the kitchen creating innovative dishes which won her several European culinary awards. While congenial host, Umberto, deals directly with guests at reception and in the main dining room, sister Patrizia bakes cakes and creates marvelous pastries. She also finds time for watercolor painting, examples of which are found throughout the inn. Breakfast is served either out in the pretty garden seen from the large windows of the dining room, or in the intimate sitting room just left of reception with large gray-stone fireplace. Newly renovated rooms upstairs with all amenities are tastefully coordinated with elegant antiques and rich fabrics. The inn is uniquely situated right next door to the beautiful park and ruins of Emperor Hadrian's villa (circa 120 A.D.) which makes it a quiet spot at night. The park is literally all yours around closing time at sunset. Take a peek at the guest book where such illustrious guests as Queen Elizabeth and John F. Kennedy have signed. Altogether a delightful combination. *Directions*: From either the A24 from Rome, or A1 from Florence or Naples, exit at Tivoli, and follow signs for Villa Adriana, below the actual city of Tivoli.

HOTEL ADRIANO **NEW**
Hosts: Cinelli family
Via di Villa Adriana 194
Tivoli (RM) 00010, Italy
Tel: (0774) 382235 Fax: (0774) 535122
7 rooms with private bathrooms, 3 suites
Lire 160,000–200,000 double B&B
All meals served
Open all year
Credit cards: MC, VS
Some English spoken
Region: Lazio

The vast Palazzetta farm, up in the hills outside the picturesque town of Todi, offers a nice combination of comfortable accommodations and excellent local fare. The Caracciolo family reside in one of the many farmhouses in the complex of 17th-century stone buildings, while guests are accommodated in the converted farmers' quarters, or in the lovely rooms in the main villa which have specially selected antiques, stenciled drawings, and generous views over the rolling countryside. The remaining guestrooms have stone interior walls, high-beamed ceilings, and terra-cotta floors appropriately complementing simple country antiques. A cozy living room with an enormous fireplace and soft floral sofas invites guests to curl up with a good book. Yet other, rather small rooms are divided between the one-story barn and house behind the restaurant. The former cattle barn is now a delightful restaurant, totally frescoed on one wall by a well-known set designer. One can also dine on the veranda overlooking green hills and distant swimming pool, enjoying a superb meal prepared by a chef formerly from a famous local restaurant. *Directions:* From Todi follow signs for Orvieto, turning left at the sign for Palazzetta and proceeding for 7 kilometers. From Orvieto, take route 448 toward Todi, watching for Palazzetta signs after the lake ends.

LA PALAZZETTA
Hosts: Ennio Caracciolo family
Localita: Asproli
Todi (PG) 06059, Italy
Tel: (075) 8853219 Fax: (075) 8853358
19 rooms with private bathrooms
Lire 130,000–160,000 double B&B
  (prices seasonal), 3-day minimum stay
All meals served
Open all year
Some English spoken
Region: Umbria

In the midst of the bucolic countryside surrounding Todi sits the refined bed and breakfast of Poggio d'Asproli. Bruno Pagliari, a sculptor with a long family history in the hotel business, transferred his family from Naples to this 19th-century stone farmhouse several years ago and has succeeded in his aim of creating elegant but comfortable surroundings to make guests feel at home. Each of the six romantic guestrooms is unique in style and decor. Rich fabrics draped at bedheads give a canopy effect with matching bedspreads and nice big bathrooms have travertine marble sinks. To the back is a large two-bedroom suite with a separate entrance. The home is filled to the brim with antiques and lovely artwork (some by Bruno's sister, Lilli) which blend in well with the stone walls, worn brick floors, and beamed ceilings. Breakfast and candlelit dinners are served either on the outside terrace or in the elegant dining room. At one end is a cozy sitting area with white sofas around an enormous fireplace. A swimming pool among the trees is a cool spot for relaxing. Daughter, Claudia, is slowly taking over the general management of the bed and breakfast. *Directions:* From Todi, follow signs for Orvieto and take a left at the sign for Izzalini. Before town, take the turning for Asproli and follow signs to the bed and breakfast.

POGGIO D'ASPROLI **NEW**
Hostess: Claudia Pagliari
Localita: Asproli
Todi (PG) 06059, Italy
Tel & fax: (075) 8853385
6 rooms, 1 suite, all with private bathrooms
Lire 200,000 double B&B
  130,000 per person half board
2-day minimum stay
Breakfast and dinner served
Open all year
English spoken well
Region: Umbria

When the Marti family from Rome came across the abandoned castle of Montegualandro six years ago, it was love at first sight—only pure passion could have driven them to tackle such an overwhelming project as the entire restoration of the property following original plans. A long winding dirt road leads one up to the walled castle's iron gates. Entering into the open circular courtyard, the main building and family residence lies to the left and immediately to the right is the long stone house, originally farmer's quarters with small tower, stable, pottery kiln, dove house, and private chapel. Four apartments have been fashioned for guests, cleverly incorporating all original architectural features. One different from the next, each has a living area with fireplace, kitchen, and bathroom and is characteristically furnished with country-style antiques. A walk up in the turreted walls gives a glimpse of the spectacular view out over olive groves (the property produces its own olive oil) to the lake. The Martis' daughter, Cristiana, takes special interest in guests needs, suggesting easy day trips from the castle and recommending favorite local restaurants. Lovely Cortona is just 10 kilometers away. *Directions*: Montegualandro is marked on most maps. Exit at Tuoro from the Perugia highway 75bis and travel towards Cortona and Castiglione. After 3 kilometers, before a curve to the left, take a small unmarked road at S. Angelo up to the castle or call from town.

CASTELLO DI MONTEGUALANDRO   **NEW**
Hosts: The Marti family
Via di Montegualandro 1
Tuoro sul Trasimeno (PG) 06069, Italy
Tel & fax: (075) 8230267
4 apartments for 2 to 4 persons
Lire 500,000–1,200,000 weekly
No meals served
Open all year
English spoken very well
Region: Umbria

La Dogana means customs house in Italian, and the fascinating history of this 16th-century building—which until 1870 served as the Papal customs house for travelers through the Grand Duchy of Tuscany—boasts visits from luminary artists such as Michelangelo, Goethe, Byron, and Stendhal. The 100-acre property belongs to young hosts Emanuele and Paola and, aside from the main villa, includes a stone farmhouse and a building near the stables across the street. In these two "extra" buildings 25 apartment-suites have been created. The guest quarters vary widely in condition, but all feature a living area, kitchen, bathroom, and sleeping accommodations for two to six people. Each apartment is unique in decor, containing mixed antiques, prints, old sofas, and wrought-iron beds. Up on a hillside, guests have a lovely view over Lake Trasimeno whose encircling highway is audible even from here. Although no meals are served, the Dogana is conveniently situated near Perugia, Cortona, and Montepulciano, where an excellent meal is a cinch to find. *Directions:* From Perugia, take N75 toward Firenze, exiting at Tuoro. Turn left at the first intersection, continuing 3 kilometers to La Dogana on the right side of the road.

LA DOGANA
Host: Marchese Emanuele de Ferrari
Via Dogana 4
Tuoro sul Trasimeno, (PG) 06069, Italy
Tel: (075) 8230158 or (0330) 280845
Fax: (075) 8230252
25 apartments
Lire 400,000–900,000 weekly
  (July & August)
No meals served
Open all year
English spoken very well
Region: Umbria

Those who have fallen in love with the enchanting countryside of Tuscany, but found its roads too well-traveled, should investigate the northern part of the Marches surrounding Urbino. The scenery is magnificent, the ancient towns perfectly preserved, and the ambiance authentic. The Blasi families, hard-working farmers, have dedicated themselves to balancing a productive farm with a bed and breakfast. The brother's side of the family tends to the fields, while Amadeo, his wife Maria, and their two sons see to the guests. Three simple terra-cotta-roofed houses make up the farm, and horses, cows, sheep, and even peacocks roam the grounds. The eight guestrooms, each with private bath, are spartan, and the decor uninspired, but the familial warmth of the hospitality, the excellent home cooking, and the value compensate. In the rustic dining room with red-checked tablecloths or on the windowed veranda overlooking the gently rolling, wooded countryside, guests indulge in Maria's spinach ravioli or hand-cut tagliatelle, fresh-baked bread, and local wine. *Directions:* From Urbino take the road to Urbania. Pass through town and follow signs for Acqualagna. After 9 kilometers turn right where indicated and follow signs up to L'Orsaiola.

L'ORSAIOLA
Hosts: Blasi families
Localita: Orsaiola
Urbania 61049 (PS) 61049, Italy
Tel: (0722) 318988
5 rooms, 2 with private bathrooms
3 apartments
Lire 65,000 double B&B
 60,000 per person half board
All meals served
Open March to Christmas
Very little English spoken
Region: Marches

Isabella and her husband came down from the Dolomite mountains to the enchanting area surrounding the town of Urbino 20 years ago and have resided there ever since. Their stone farmhouse is situated on the summit of one of the rolling green hills that characterize this bucolic countryside here. Before starting the bed and breakfast, Isabella had her own esthetician business and continues to practice that trade by offering her guests facials and massages with her own natural herbal creams; hence the name *Beauty Farm*. Guests are made to feel right at home at the Giuriattis', sharing the spacious living room, well-furnished with family antiques, and dining room where meals are enjoyed all together at a big table. As the cook is from Sardinia, specialties served are not specific to the Marches. However, one regional delicacy often figures in the dishes, since part of the farm is a white-truffle reserve. Upstairs are found the five guestrooms, each with bath, casually and individually arranged using a mix of old and new furniture and personal family items. Besides the beautiful university town of Urbino, there are other interesting side trips to nearby San Leo and the Republic of San Marino. *Directions:* From Urbino (10 kilometers) take route 73 toward Arezzo. After Montesoffio turn right at Pozzuolo.

THE BEAUTY FARM
Hostess: Isabella Giuriatti
Localita: Pozzuolo 60-Montesoffio
Urbino, (PS) 61029, Italy
Tel: (0722) 57183
5 rooms with private bathrooms
Lire 85,000 per person half board
Breakfast and dinner served
Open all year
Some English spoken
Region: Marches

The Gasthof Obereggen, located in the Ega Valley is very simple, but its location and price are hard to match. The inn is situated on the side of a hill overlooking a gorgeous valley in one of the most beautiful mountain regions of northeastern Italy. The town of Obereggen is a ski resort and the lift is just a few minutes' walk away. From the sun-drenched deck, which extends generously from the hotel, there is an absolutely glorious vista across the meadows to the mountains. Behind the hotel even more majestic peaks rise jaggedly into the sky. Inside there is a cozy dining room with hunting trophies lining the walls and a typical tiled stove against one wall to keep the room toasty on a cold day. The inn has twelve basically uninspired bedrooms, with those on the second floor opening out onto balconies with lovely views. The Gasthof's greatest asset is Signora Pichler who runs her little inn with warmth and gaiety. She speaks no English, but her hospitality overcomes all language barriers, and her abundant and delicious home-style cooking speaks to all who love to eat. *Directions:* Obereggen is almost impossible to find on any map, although the Val d'Ega and the town of Ega (San Floriano on some maps) are usually indicated. Obereggen is 3 kilometers south of Nova Levante and 25 kilometers southeast of Bolzano.

GASTHOF OBEREGGEN
Hosts: Pichler family
Obereggen (San Floriano)
Val d'Ega (BZ) 39050, Italy
Tel: (0471) 615722
12 rooms, several with private bathrooms
Lire 70,000 per person half board
All meals served
Closed May to June
No English spoken (German)
Region: Trentino-Alto Adige

Varenna is a quaint little village sitting halfway up Lake Como's eastern edge. It is situated at the point where the car-ferryboats cross over to the other side of the lake to Menaggio. In the main piazza lakeside is the family-run Olivedo hotel with its pale yellow façade. Time seems to have stood still within its old-fashioned interior. The reception area and side bar are dressed with faded floral wallpaper, scattered antiques, and a large grandfather clock chiming the hour. Off to the other side of the reception area is a dining room/restaurant with its simple frescoes, serving all meals. A curved stairway takes guests up to the 19 rooms most with en-suite bathroom and lake views. These are decorated simply with grandmother's furniture and old prints. There is no need to worry about noise since traffic is not allowed in the piazza. Bathrooms are being progressively renewed and added. *Directions:* From the Como branch of the lake, head north on either side of lake and take the ferry over from either Bellagio or Menaggio.

OLIVEDO
Hosts: Colombo family
Piazza Martiri 4
Varenna (CO) 22050, Italy
Tel: (0341) 830115
19 rooms, 10 with private bathrooms
Lire 80,000–125,000 double B&B
All meals served
Open all year
Very little English spoken
Region: Lombardy

With its steady flow of year-round tourism, Venice is decidedly Italy's most expensive city. Although its list of bed-and-breakfast-like hotels (small, family-run) is seemingly endless, finding those with a bed-and-breakfast price range is a bit more challenging. The Bel Sito fits right into the extensive mid-range category. Centrally situated in a quiet corner of the square behind the elegant Gritti Hotel, near St. Mark's, the cheery yellow façade, outdoor café, rooftop terrace, and cascading geraniums at the windows make it an instant charmer. For such a relatively small hotel, it offers plenty of communal spaces for guests including a large reception area decorated in typical Venetian style, long mirrored breakfast room, and cozy bar. The four rooms in the annex with canal view and total silence are the most desirable, if not the two front rooms with small balconies. Dotted with antiques, the carpeted rooms, each with small bathrooms, vary greatly in decor, some being more worn at the edges than others. Air conditioning is available at an extra daily charge. *Directions*: Take the No. 1 water bus to stop 13, Santa Maria del Giglio, and head straight into the square.

HOTEL BEL SITO **NEW**
Owner: Luigi Gino Serafini
San Marco 2517
Campo Santa Maria del Giglio
Venice, 30124, Italy
Tel: (041) 5223365/5223394 Fax: (041) 5204083
35 rooms with private bathrooms
Lire 230,000 double B&B
Breakfast only
Open all year
Credit cards: all major
Some English spoken
Region: Veneto

Around the corner from the Santa Maria del Giglio square, sitting on a small private canal's edge is the small and intimate San Moise hotel, named after the nearby church. Hospitality is a tradition in the Donzello family who owns three other hotels in Venice and hostess and owner Signora Irvin obviously takes pride in her work as seen in the attention to detail of her newly renovated accommodation. Upon entering the pale-yellow 15th-century building one finds the reception desk and the stairway up to the guestrooms immediately on the right. To the left is the very small but cozy combination lounge/breakfast room decorated with elegant antiques, Murano glass chandeliers, and walls covered with soft-pink flocked fabric. Bedrooms on the second and third floors are in the same vein with variations in the color scheme, some having the advantage of a partial canal view without the usual noise. Rooms are fully equipped with all amenities including air conditioning and you can even leave your gondola at the private dock! Directions: Take the No. 1 water bus to stop 15, San Marco; walk straight up to Calle 22 Marzo and turn left. Pass the church on the left and turn right at the sign for the hotel.

HOTEL SAN MOISE **NEW**
Hostess: Irvin Donzello
San Marco 2058
Venice 30124, Italy
Tel: (041)5203755 Fax: (041) 5210670
16 rooms with private bathrooms
Lire 283,000 double B&B
Breakfast only
Open all year
Credit cards: all major
English spoken well
Region: Veneto

Places to Stay

With just eleven rooms paired up throughout the six-floor building, (luckily with an elevator), the intimate San Stefano resembles a tower of sorts. The compact hotel, originally a private home, is right in the middle of the large, open Santo Stefano square which leads to St. Mark's on one side and to the bridge for Accademia on the other. An outdoor patio with bordering plants adorns the entrance leading to the bright and cheerful lobby with its pale-yellow beamed ceiling, faux marble walls, and a reception desk painted with 18th-century canal scenes. Just beyond is a miniature breakfast room for days when bad weather does not permit having it served out in the piazza. Touches of elegance follow through in the room decor with ornate glass lamps, gilded mirrors, and painted furniture, plus immaculate bathrooms. A sweet little hotel, but not for those who suffer from claustrophobia. This hotel provides all amenities including air conditioning at an extra charge. *Directions*: Take water bus No. 1 to the Accademia stop. Pass over the bridge and straight into Campo Santo Stefano.

HOTEL SANTO STEFANO **NEW**
Owner: Signor Gazzola
San Marco 2957
Venice 30124, Italy
Tel: (041) 5200166 Fax: (041) 5224460
11 rooms with private bathrooms adjacent
Lire 160,000–200,000 double B&B
Breakfast only
Open all year
Credit cards: all major
English spoken well
Region: Veneto

The Hotel Torino is yet another typically Venetian accommodation in style, dimension, and price level. But what sets it apart from the rest is its rich interiors, intact from its days as a 15th-century palace. The small reception area, stairway leading up to the 20 rooms, intimate salon, and upstairs breakfast room (although breakfast is normally served in the rooms) are filled with an eclectic mixture of museum-quality pieces and artwork. The comfortable bedrooms are tastefully appointed with antiques, fabric-covered walls, and Venetian glass chandeliers. They either face the back or look out through leaded glass windows onto the busy Calle delle Ostreghe street connecting St. Mark's square with Campo Santo Stefano which leads over the bridge to the Accademia and P. Guggenheim Collection. The street is full of small interesting boutiques and artisans' shops. Amidst this historic ambiance are all modern amenities including air conditioning. Book well in advance. *Directions*: Take water bus No. 1 to the Santa Maria del Giglio stop.

HOTEL TORINO **NEW**
Owner: Claudio Vecchiato
Calle delle Ostreghe 2356
Venice 30124, Italy
Tel: (041) 5205222 Fax: (041) 5228227
20 rooms with private bathrooms
Lire 190,000–260,000 double B&B
Breakfast only
Open all year
Credit cards: all major
Some English spoken
Region: Veneto

With admirable determination and family pride, Alessandro and his new bride, Deborah, took on the task of renovating and running the hotel property which has been part of the family for three generations. They deserve great credit since they are more concerned with providing warm hospitality and attention to guests' needs than with keeping up with Venice's inflated hotel rates. Indeed, this is the only accommodation under 200,000 lire that met our standards. The spacious and luminous reception area with white travertine floors is a welcome oasis amid the city's more cramped hotels, bustling squares, and crowded narrow streets. Although only a three-minute walk from the Guggenheim collection and Accademia, it has the feeling of being away from the mainstream traffic. The front rooms with water views (but noise) maintain an original flavor of simplicity with parquet floors and matching wood furniture, velvet rose-colored chairs, and new bathrooms. Air conditioning is being installed 'in rooms this year. A Continental breakfast is served either in the breakfast room with country accents or out on the large front dock terrace where you can watch the boats going by. *Directions*: Take the No. 52 water bus to Zattere, then follow the quay to the right where you will see the hotel terrace.

PENSIONE LA CALCINA   **NEW**
Hosts: Alessandro & Deborah Szemere
Dorsoduro 780
Venice 30123, Italy
Tel: (041) 5206466 Fax: (041) 5227045
40 rooms with private bathrooms
Lire 180,000 double B&B
Breakfast only
Open all year
Credit cards: all major
English spoken well
Region: Veneto

At first glance the exterior of the Pensione Seguso appears quite bland: a rather boxy affair with few of the elaborate architectural enhancements so frequently evident in Venice. Inside, however, the *pensione* radiates warmth and charm, with Oriental rugs setting off antique furniture and an heirloom silver service. The hotel is located on the "left bank" of Venice: across the Grand Canal from the heart of the tourist area, about a 15-minute walk to St. Mark's Square (or only a few minutes by ferry from the Accademia boat stop). For several generations the hotel has been in the Seguso family, which provides a homey ambiance for guests who do not demand luxury. In front there is a miniature terrace harboring a few umbrella-shaded tables. Several of the bedrooms have views of the canal (although these are the noisiest due to canal traffic). Being a simple *pensione*, most of the rooms share a bathroom, so if you are looking for hotel amenities, Seguso may not be your "cup of tea." The pleasant surprise is that the value-conscious tourist can stay here with breakfast and dinner included for the price of a room alone at most Venice hotels. *Directions:* The Seguso is a ten-minute walk from the Accademia boat stop.

PENSIONE SEGUSO
Hosts: Lorenzo Seguso family
Grand Canal Zattere 779
Venice 30123, Italy
Tel: (041) 5286858 Fax: (041) 5222340
36 rooms, 19 with private bathrooms
Lire 140,000 per person half board
Breakfast and dinner served
Open March to November
Credit cards: all major
English spoken well
Region: Veneto

Just 20 kilometers from the Swiss border, halfway along the shore of Lake Maggiore, at the point where the road curves back down to Verbania, is a farmhouse ideally situated 700 meters above the lake. It commands a 360-degree view which includes the Alps and Lakes Mergozzo, Monate, Varese, and Maggiore with its miniature Borromeo islands (accessible by ferryboat). A long 5-kilometer road winds its way up to the turn-of-the-century house with tower. Energetic and friendly hostess, Iside Minotti, and her family run the inn and rustic restaurant, which is busy spot in the summer when locals come up to dine and take advantage of the cooler air and the spectacular view. Menu ingredients come directly from the vegetable garden and orchards to the kitchen, where sumptuous local specialties are prepared. Even Papa Minotti gets involved and can be heard singing folk songs in front of the open grill. The 25-acre farm includes riding stables, and the bed and breakfast can also arrange for a helicopter from Fondotoce for a breathtakingly scenic ride over the lake. Six basic and modern, though comfortable, double rooms with bath are available for overnight guests. *Directions:* Before Verbania, at Pallanza, take Via Azari to Monterosso (left turnoff) up 5 kilometers of winding road that includes over 40 hairpin bends.

IL MONTEROSSO
Hostess: Iside Minotti
Cima Monterosso-C.P. 13
Verbania (NO) 28048, Italy
Tel: (0323) 556510 Fax: (0323) 556718
6 rooms with private bathrooms
Lire 70,000 double B&B
* 65,000 per person half board*
All meals served
Open all year
Some English spoken
Region: Piedmont

With great finesse, determined Sandra and Paolo, an editor, managed to purchase this magnificent Renaissance villa—no easy feat, considering the 400-acre property had been in one family for 700 years. The pale-yellow villa with handsome lawns and surrounding cypress woods commands a spectacular view over the immense valley and Mugello mountain range. This is the area north of Florence known for its concentration of Medici villas. The eight guestrooms in the villa have been restored to their original splendor, with high Florentine woodworked ceilings, carefully selected antiques, and delightful blue-and-white-tiled bathrooms. The honeymoon suite features a grand gold-crowned red canopy bed. The entry leads to the frescoed dining rooms where original combinations of fresh local produce are served with great attention to detail, accompanied by an excellent selection of wines. Recent additions include nine new rooms on the third floor of the villa, a lovely swimming pool, and horse stables. Villa Campestri offers refined and romantic accommodations in the vicinity of Florence. *Directions:* Exit at Barberino di Mugello from the A1 autostrada and follow signs for S. Pietro Asieve, then Cardetole, then Sagginale, and finally up the road on the right to Vicchio—35 kilometers from Florence.

VILLA CAMPESTRI
Host: Sandra Cesari & Paolo Pasquali
Localita: Campestri 19/22
Vicchio di Mugello (FI) 50039, Italy
Tel: (055) 8490107 Fax: (055) 8490108
17 rooms with private bathrooms
Lire 200,000 double B&B
* 130,000 per person half board*
Breakfast & dinner served
Open April to December
Credit cards: MC, VS
English spoken well
Region: Tuscany

On the northern outskirts of the beautiful city of Treviso is a busy farm which was once a convent. The long building has been made into several residences, one belonging to the two Milani brothers, where a restaurant and six bedrooms have been fashioned for guests. All of the bedrooms have private baths, and their decor is very much in keeping with the simple country style of the farm. Typical Venetian antiques enhance the rooms, which also feature homey touches such as white-lace curtains and soft floral armchairs. Guests can observe the wine production taking place on the farm and are also welcome to take horses out on excursions, or take riding lessons if desired. The popular restaurant prides itself on serving local specialties prepared with the farm's fresh produce and game. The restaurant with its large, open central hearth, is a welcoming gathering spot, decorated with lots of pictures, brass pots, pink tablecloths, and fresh flowers. Although the immediate surrounding flat countryside is the not most inspiring, this a great base for visiting Venice, Padova, Vianza, and Verona. *Directions:* From Venice (34 kilometers away), take route N13 through Treviso, and on toward Villorba, turning left at the sign for the Podere. Or exit at Treviso Nord from the A27.

PODERE DEL CONVENTO
Host: Renzo Milani
Via IV Novembre 16
Villorba (TV) 31050, Italy
Tel: (0422) 920044
6 rooms with private bathrooms
Lire 80,000 double B&B
70,000 per person half board
All meals served
Open all year
Credit cards: AX, VS
No English spoken
Region: Veneto

Ninni Bacchi has done wonders in transforming her family's 300-acre tobacco and grain farm (just 38 kilometers from Orvieto) into a very comfortable bed and breakfast in an area that was once the heart of the Etruscan civilization. Arriving guests are warmly received by manager, Monica, in the luminous, open living room furnished with antiques surrounding a grand fireplace. Downstairs is the large, arcaded restaurant dating back to the 15th century, where guests can enjoy the fine cuisine of the Lazio region or dine outdoors by the saltwater pool. The five bedrooms off the courtyard in the main house have the most character with architectural features intact, while the remaining 15 suites are lined up in two cottage-like wings, and are more spacious and modern in decor. A good job has been done with the landscaping, pleasingly distracting the eye from the rather bland and flat countryside hereabouts. Unfortunately, the commercial zone of Viterbo is slowly invading the area—don't be alarmed by the unattractive approach. Tennis, biking and horseback riding, plus the nearby thermal spa are some of the activities available. Directions: From Rome (120 kilometers away) follow signs for Viterbo. Take the Cassia road north of Viterbo for 3 kilometers toward Montefiascone, turning right at the Rinaldone sign.

RESIDENCE RINALDONE
Hostess: Ninni Bacchi
Strada Rinaldone, 9-S.S. Cassia km 86
Viterbo 01100, Italy
Tel: (0761) 352137 Fax: (0761) 353116
5 rooms, 15 suites with private bathrooms
Lire 145,000 double B&B
2-day minimum stay
All meals served
Open April to November
Credit cards: all major
Some English spoken
Region: Lazio

Given the unbearable August heat in most parts of the country, and the inevitably overcrowded conditions at the seaside resorts during that month, it is small wonder that the cooler elevations of the Alps and Dolomites have become a favorite vacation destinations for Italian families. In addition to offering the ideal atmosphere for relaxation and recharging, they offer invigorating fresh mountain air, numerous outdoor activities, spectacular scenery, and, best of all, the least expensive "getaway" available in the country. The darling Merlhof bed and breakfast is owned and operated by the Kompatschers, who have created seven guestrooms within their family home in the town of Fié. The traditional, Tyrolean-style white-and-dark-wood dwelling has geraniums cascading brightly from each windowsill, and looks directly onto Sciliar mountain at the back. The guestrooms are simply furnished with light-pine wood beds and side tables, and only one has its own bathroom. The breakfast room overlooks the town and a small swimming pool, which is a welcome feature indeed on hot summer afternoons or after a day of hiking. *Directions:* Exit at Bolzano Nord from the Verona-Brennero autostrada. Follow signs for Siusi and Völs (also called Fié) and, at the main intersection, turn right to Merlhof.

MERLHOF
Hosts: Maria Kompatscher family
Via Sciliar 14
Fié allo Sciliar (Völs) (BZ) 39050, Italy
Tel: (0471) 725092
7 rooms, 1 with private bathroom
Lire 30,000 per person B&B
Breakfast only
Open all year
No English spoken (German)
Region: Trentino-Alto Adige

Key Map

Map 1

AUSTRIA

AUSTRIA

38

A22

Barbian

Bressanone
(Brixen)

49

49

Sexton (Sesto)

BOLZANO
(Bolzen)

Castelrotto

Völs (Fié)

51

Tiers (Tires)

48

CORTINA

38

48

48

42

42

Val d' Ega

51

48

Cavalese

ALTO ADIGE

A22

51

● Places to Stay

○ Orientation/
Sightseeing

BELLUNO

a	b
c	d

Quadrants

TRENTO

47

50

Feltre

Map 2

Map 3

SWITZERLAND

LUGANO

Menaggio

Lake Como

Verbania

Lake Maggiore

Lake Lugano

San Fedele
d'Intelvi

Varenna

Stresa

Argegno

Bellagio

LECCO

COMO

Caprino
Bergamasco

Alzano Lombardo

A9

BERGAMO

Malpensa
Airport

A8

A4

Biella

Candelo

LOMBARDY

Mottalciata

A26

MILAN
(Milano)

Linate
Airport

Novara

A7

A8

A1

PAVIA

Cremona

ALESSANDRIA

A21

Map 4

PIACENZA

A21

Tortona

Borgo Priolo

● Places to Stay

○ Orientation/
   Sightseeing

a	b
c	d
  Quadrants

Map 5

Map 6

EMILIA-ROMAGNA

○ FERRARA

MODENA ○

● Castelfranco Emilia

● BOLOGNA

ADRIATIC SEA

Monte San Pietro ●

● Castel Guelfo

○ RAVENNA

Faenza ○

● Brisighella

○ Forli

● Places to Stay

○ Orientation/ Sightseeing

| a | b | Quadrants
|---|---|
| c | d |

● Roggio

Borgo San Lorenzo

○ Vicchio di Mugello

● Montiano

Cantagallo ●

Pistoia ○

● Portico di Romagna

Prato ●

Sesto Fiorentino ●

LUCCA ○

● Baccchereto

● Castiglioni di Rufina

● Montevettolini

Rufina ● Pomino

TUSCANY

○ PISA

FLORENCE (Firenze)

Map 7

Map 8

Map 9

Map 10

Map 11

Isole Tremiti

Gargano

APULIA

Barletta

BARI

Monopoli

E58

Pezze di Greco

Ostuni

San Vito dei Normanni

Potenza

Matera

407

A3/E1

TARANTO

BRINDISI

Avetrana

LECCE

Galatone

Maratea

CROTONE

A3/E1

TROPEA

A3/E1

Sicily

REGGIO

Map 12

● Places to Stay

○ Orientation/
    Sightseeing

a	b
c	d

Quadrants

211

Sicily

Stromboli

Filicudi
Salina
Alicudi
Lipari
Vulcano

MESSINA

MILAZZO

TRAPANI
Erice
Scopello
PALERMO
CEFALÙ
S. Stefano
A20
Villa San
Giovanni
"Toe" of Italy

Egadi Isles
Segesta
113
Pettineo
A18
TAORMINA

MARSALA
A29
Gangi
Fiumefreddo
Mount Etna
National
Park

Menfi
Gangivecchio

Sciacca
A19
Misterbianco
CATANIA

Selinunte
ENNA

AGRIGENTO
Piazza
Armerina
417

Rome
640
114

115
SYRACUSE (Siracusa)

115

● Places to Stay

○ Orientation/
  Sightseeing

▲ Archaeological sites

a | b Quadrants
c | d

Map 13

Valle d'Aosta

Piedmont

Milan

Lombardy

Trentino-Alto-Adige

Veneto

Friuli-Venezia-Giulia

Venice

Emila-Romagna

Genoa

Liguria

Florence

Tuscany

Marches

Umbria

CORSICA (France)

ROME

Lazio

Abruzzo

Molise

Sardinia

Campania

Naples

Basilicata

Bari

Apulia

Cagliari

Calabria

Palermo

Sicily

Regions of Italy

213

Bed and Breakfasts by Region

Apulia

Avetrana, Bosco di Mudonato
Galatone, Masseria Lo Prieno
Monopoli, Masseria Curatori
Ostuni, Masseria Lo Spagnulo
Pezzi di Greco, Masseria Salamina
San Vito dei Normanni, Tenuta Deserto

Campania

Capri, La Minerva
    Villa Krupp
    Villa Vuotto
Positano, Casa Cosenza
    La Fenice
Ravello, Villa Amore
    Villa Maria

Emilia-Romagna

Bologna, Hotel Orologio
Brisighella, Il Palazzo
Castel Guelfo, Locanda Solarola
Castelfranco Emilia, Villa Gaidello
Monte San Pietro, Tenuta Bonzara
Montiano, Le Radici
Portico di Romagna, Albergo al Vecchio Convento
Salsomaggiore Terme, Antica Torre

Lazio

Orte, La Chiocciola
Ponza, Isola di, I Due Pini
Rome, Casa Stefazio
    Hotel Due Torri
    Fontana Hotel
    Hotel Locarno
    Hotel Teatro di Pompeo
    Hotel Venezia
    Hotel Villa del Parco
Rome (Boccea), Tenuta Santa Rufina
Tivoli, Hotel Adriano
Viterbo, Residence Rinaldone

Liguria

Castiglione Chiavarese, Monte Pu
Santa Margherita Ligure, Gnocchi
Tavarone di Maissana, Giandriale
Tellaro, Locanda Miranda

Lombardy

Alzano Lombardo, Cascina Grumello
Borgo Priolo, Castello di Stefanago
Caprino Bergamasco, Ombria
Milan, Hotel Regina
Porto Mantovano, Villa Schiarino Lena
San Fedele d'Intelvi, Villa Simplicitas

Lombardy (cont.)
Varenna, Olivedo

Marches
Massignano, La Biancarda
Montefiore d'Aso, La Campana
Portonovo, Hotel Emilia
    Fortino Napoleonico
Sirolo, Locanda Rocco
Urbania, L'Orsaiola
Urbino (Montesoffio), The Beauty Farm

Piedmont
Alba, Cascina Reine
Candelo, La Mandria
Canelli, La Luna e i Falo
Mottalciata, Il Mompolino
San Marzano Oliveto, Antica Fattoria del Colle
    La Viranda
Verbania, Il Monterosso

Sicily
Fiumefreddo, Borgo Valerio
Gangivecchio, Tenuta Gangivecchio
Menfi, Ravida
Misterbianco, Alcala
Pettineo, Casa Migliaca
Scopello, Casale Degli Olivi
    Pensione Tranchina

Siracusa, Limoneto
Taormina, Villa Schuler

Trentino-Alto Adige
Barbian, Bad Dreikirchen
Castelrotto, Marmsolerhof
Castelrotto (Osvaldo), Tschotscherhof
Tiers (Tires), Veraltenhof
Val d'Ega-Obereggen, Gasthof Obereggen
Völs (Fié), Merlhof

Tuscany
Ansedonia, La Locanda di Ansedonia
    Grazia
Bacchereto, Fattoria di Bacchereto
Bagnone, Villa Mimosa
Barberino Val d'Elsa, Fattoria Casa Sola
    Il Paretaio
    La Chiara di Prumiano
    La Spinosa
Bettolle, Locanda la Bandita
Cantagallo, Ponte Alla Villa
Casole d'Elsa, Podere Capretto
Castelnuovo Berardenga, Podere San Quirico
    Borga Villa a Sesta
Castiglioni di Rufina, La Sosta ai Busini
Ciciano, Casa Italia
Cortona, Il Falconiere
    Stoppiacce

Tuscany (cont.)
Cortona, Villa Il Bacchino
Florence, Hotel Aprile
    Hotel Ariele
    Hotel Desiree
    Hotel Hermitage
    La Residenza
    Hotel Silla
    Hotel Splendor
Gaiole in Chianti, Castello di Tornano
Galluzzo (Florence), La Fattoressa
Giogoli (Florence), Il Milione
Greve in Chianti, Casa Nova
Le Valli (Incisa Val d'Arno), San Niccolo d'Olmeto
Lucolena, Locanda Borgo Antico
Manciano, Campigliola Country Club
Mercatale Val di Pesa, Salvadonica
Modanella (Serre di Rapolano), Godiolo
    Castello di Modanella
Montefiridolfi, Fattoria La Loggia
Montemerano, Villa Acquaviva
Montemerano (Poderi di), Le Fontanelle
    Locanda Laudomia
Montevettolini, Villa Lucia
Pienza, La Saracina
Pomino, Fattoria Petrognano
Prato, Villa Rucellai di Canneto
Radda in Chianti, Azienda Agricola Vergelli

Radda in Chianti, Le Selve II
    Podere Terreno
    Podere Val delle Corti
    Torre Canvalle
Radicofani, La Palazzina
Ripa d'Orcia, Castello di Ripa d'Orcia
Roggio, Azienda Coletti
Rosia, Montestigliano
San Gimignano, Casanova di Pescille
    Casolare di Libbiano
    Podere Villuzza
San Rocco a Pilli, Fattoria di Cavaglioni
Sarteano, La Sovana
Saturnia, Villa Clodia
Sesto Fiorentino, Podere Novelleto
Tavarnelle Val di Pesa, Podere Sovigliano
Terontola, Residenza San Andrea al Farinaio
Vicchio di Mugello, Villa Campestri

Umbria

Armenzano (Assisi), Le Silve di Armenzano
Assisi (Capodacqua), Malvarina
Assisi (Tordibetto di), Podere la Fornace
Baschi, Pomurlo Vecchio
Bovara di Trevi, Casa Giulia
Calvi dell'Umbria, Casale San Martino
Castel del Piano Umbro, Villa Aureli
Colle San Paolo (Panicale), Villa di Montesolare
Deruta, Antica Fattoria del Colle

Umbria (cont.)
Ficulle, La Casella
Gaifana, Villa della Cupa
Mengara (Gubbio), Oasi Verde
Montecastello di Vibio, Fattoria di Vibio
Niccone (Umbertide), La Maridiana
Orvieto, Fattoria la Cacciata
    Villa Ciconia
Ospedaletto (San Venanzo), Borgo Spante
Paciano, Locanda della Rocca
Ponte Pattoli, Il Covone
Solfagnano, La Torre di Bagnara
Spoleto, Residenza Vaita de Domo
Titignano, Fattoria Titignano
Todi, La Palazzetta
    Poggio d'Asproli
Tuoro sul Trasimeno, Castello di Montegualandro
    La Dogana

Valle d'Aosta
Entreves (Courmayeur), La Grange

Veneto
Barbarano Vicentino, Il Castello
Levada di Piombino Dese, Gargan
Monselice, Fattoria Savellon Molini
San Ambrogio Valpolicella, Ca'Verde

Venice, Hotel Bel Sito
    Hotel San Moise
    Hotel Santo Stefano
    Hotel Torino
    Pensione La Calcina
    Pensione Seguso
Villorba, Podere del Convento

Index

F

Falconiere, Il, Cortona, 68
Farm Names, Regional, 14
Fattoria Casa Sola, Barberino Val d'Elsa, 37
Fattoria del Colle, Antica, San Marzano Oliveto, 153
Fattoria di Bacchereto, 34
Fattoria di Cavaglioni, San Rocco a Pilli, 155
Fattoria di Vibio, Montecastello di Vibio, 100
Fattoria la Cacciata, Orvieto, 111
Fattoria la Loggia, Montefiridolfi in Chianti, 102
Fattoria Petrognano, Pomino, 118
Fattoria Savellon Molini, Monselice, 98
Fattoria Titignano, Titignano, 178
Fenice, La, Positano, 126
Ficulle
    La Casella, 73
Fié allo Sciliar-Völs
    Merlhof, 198
Finding Your Bed and Breakfast, 13
    Directions, 13
    Transfers into Cities, 13
Fiumefreddo, Sicily
    Borgo Valerio, 161
Florence
    Hotel Aprile, 74
    Hotel Ariele, 75
    Hotel Desiree, 76
    Hotel Hermitage, 77
    Hotel Silla, 79
    Hotel Splendor, 80
    La Residenza, 78
Florence-Galluzzo
    La Fattoressa, 84
Florence-Giogoli
    Il Milione, 85

Fontana Hotel, Rome, 140
Fontanelle, Le, Montemerano, 104
Food, 5
    Meals Offered, 6
Fornace, La, Podere, Assisi (Tordibetto di), 32
Fortino Napoleonico, Portonovo, 124
Franchini, Nicole, 11

G

Gaidello, Villa, Castelfranco Emilia, 59
Gaifana
    Villa Della Cupa, 81
Gaiole in Chianti
    Castello di Tornano, 82
Galatone
    Masseria lo Prieno, 83
Galluzzo (Florence)
    La Fattoressa, 84
Gangivecchio, Sicily
    Tenuta Gangivecchio, 162
Gargan, Levada di Piombino Dese, 88
Gasthof Obereggen, Val d'Ega, 186
Giandriale, Tavarone di Maissana, 174
Giogoli (Florence)
    Il Milione, 85
Giulia, Casa, Bovara di Trevi, 46
Gnocchi, Santa Margherita, 157
Godiolo, Modanella (Serre di Rapolano), 95
Grange, La, Entreves (Courmayeur), 72
Grazia, Ansedonia, 28
Greve in Chianti
    Casa Nova, 86
Grumello, Cascina, Alzano Lombardo, 27
Gubbio-Mengara
    Oasi Verde, 92

HIDDEN TREASURES OF ITALY
Reservation Request Form

Name(s) of traveler(s):_____

Total number in party: _____   Number of children: _____   Ages: _____

Address: _____

_____

Tel: _____

Fax: _____

B&B name and location: _____

Second choice: _____

Type of accommodation: single _____   double _____   triple _____   apt._____

Dates desired: (Arrival) _____   (Departure) _____

Number of nights: _____

Meal plan: B&B _____   half board _____   full board _____   does not apply _____

Special Requests:

Hidden Treasures of Italy, 934 Elmwood Avenue, Wilmette IL 60091, USA
Tel: (847) 853-1312 Fax: (847) 853-1340

HIDDEN TREASURES OF ITALY

Hotel/Bed & Breakfast Booking Service

You may conveniently reserve any of the bed and breakfasts in this guide through Hidden Treasures of Italy's booking service. Car rentals and special interest tours (cooking classes, wine and garden tours, or horseback riding excursions) for small groups can also be arranged. Simply copy (as many times as necessary) and fill out the reservation-request form opposite this page and fax or mail it along with a $35 booking fee per reservation to:

HIDDEN TREASURES OF ITALY
934 Elmwood Avenue
Wilmette, IL 60091, USA
Tel: (847) 853-1312   Fax: (847) 853-1340
From Europe: Tel & fax: (Italy) 39-6-3052537

Upon confirmation of your request(s), exact rates with current exchange rate will be quoted and full prepayment by check, Visa or MasterCard will be required within 15 days from the date of notification. After receipt of payment, a written voucher will be issued to you to present to the hotel upon arrival. A **two-night minimum** stay is required per hotel/bed and breakfast.

CANCELLATION AND CHANGE POLICY
We will do our best to accommodate changes in dates or hotel choice, however this can never be guaranteed. Each additional request will require a supplementary $35 booking fee. Full refund of prepayment (excluding the booking fee) will be given up to 30 days prior to arrival date. No refund will be made within 30 days of your arrival. Booking fee is refundable **only** in the case where neither first nor second choices are available.

Cancellation insurance is strongly recommended

We Love to Hear from Karen Brown's Readers

ACCOLADES: We'd love to hear which accommodations you have especially enjoyed—even the shortest of notes is greatly appreciated. It is reassuring to know that places we recommend meet with your approval.

COMPLAINTS: Please let us know when a place we recommend fails to live up to the standards you have come to expect from Karen Brown. Constructive criticism is greatly appreciated. We sometimes make a mistake, places change, or go downhill. Your letters influence us to re-evaluate a listing.

RECOMMENDATIONS: If you have a favorite hideaway that you would like to recommend, please write to us. Give us a feel for the place, if possible send us a brochure and photographs (which we regret we cannot return). Convince us that on our next research trip, your discovery deserves a visit. All accommodations included in our guides are ones we have seen and enjoyed. Many of our finest selections are those that readers have discovered—wonderful places we would never have found on our own.

Please send information to:

KAREN BROWN'S GUIDES
Post Office Box 70
San Mateo, California 94401, USA
Telephone (415) 342-9117 Fax (415) 342-9153

SEAL COVE INN—LOCATED IN THE SAN FRANCISCO AREA

Karen Brown Herbert (best known as author of the Karen Brown's Guides) and her husband, Rick, have put 19 years of experience into reality and opened their own superb hideaway, Seal Cove Inn. Spectacularly set amongst wild flowers and bordered by towering cypress trees, Seal Cove Inn looks out to the ocean over acres of county park: an oasis where you can enjoy secluded beaches, explore tidepools, watch frolicking seals, and follow the tree-lined path that traces the windswept ocean bluffs. Country antiques, original watercolors, flower-laden cradles, rich fabrics, and the gentle ticking of grandfather clocks create the perfect ambiance for a foggy day in front of the crackling log fire. Each bedroom is its own haven with a cozy sitting area before a wood-burning fireplace and doors opening onto a private balcony or patio with views to the distant ocean. Moss Beach is a 35-minute drive south of San Francisco, 6 miles north of the picturesque town of Half Moon Bay, and a few minutes from Princeton harbor with its colorful fishing boats and restaurants. Seal Cove Inn makes a perfect base for whale-watching, salmon-fishing excursions, day trips to San Francisco, exploring the coast, or, best of all, just a romantic interlude by the sea, time to relax and be pampered. Karen and Rick look forward to the pleasure of welcoming you to their hideaway by the sea.

Seal Cove Inn, 221 Cypress Avenue, Moss Beach, California, 94038, USA
Telephone: (415) 728-7325   Fax: (415) 728-4116

Be a Karen Brown's Preferred Reader

If you would like to be the first to know when new editions of Karen Brown's Guides go to press, and also to be included in any special promotions, simply send us your name and address. We encourage you to buy new editions and throw away the old ones so that you don't miss a wealth of wonderful new discoveries or run the risk of staying in places that no longer meet our standards—you'll be glad you did. We cover the miles searching for special places so that you don't have to spend your valuable vacation time doing so.

Name _____

Street _____

Town _____ State _____ Zip _____

Telephone: _____ Fax: _____

Please send information to:

KAREN BROWN'S GUIDES
Post Office Box 70
San Mateo, California 94401, USA
Telephone (415) 342-9117   Fax (415) 342-9153

NICOLE FRANCHINI, author of *Italy: Charming Bed & Breakfasts,* was born in Chicago and raised in a bilingual family, her father being Italian. She received a B.A. degree in languages from William Smith College and the Sorbonne, Paris, and has been residing in Italy for the past 12 years. Currently living outside Rome with husband, Carlo, and daughter, Livia, she runs her own travel consulting business, Hidden Treasures of Italy, which organizes specialized group and individual itineraries. Nicole also represents several hotels and bed and breakfasts.

ELISABETTA FRANCHINI, the talented artist responsible for the illustrations in *Italy: Charming Bed & Breakfasts,* lives in her hometown of Chicago where she paints predominantly European landscapes and architectural scenes. On her annual trip to Italy she enjoys accompanying her sister, Nicole, on her travel research. A Smith College graduate in Art History and French Literature, Elisabetta has exhibited extensively in the Chicago area for the past 12 years, and has had shows in Miami, New York, and San Francisco.

JANN POLLARD, the artist responsible for the beautiful painting on the cover of this guide, has studied art since childhood, and is well-known for her outstanding impressionistic-style watercolors which she has exhibited in numerous juried shows, winning many awards. Jann travels frequently to Europe (using Karen Brown's guides) where she loves to paint historical buildings. Jann lives in Burlingame, California, with her husband, Gene.

NOTES